The Nature Way

CORBIN HARNEY
The Nature Way

As told to and edited by Alex Purbrick

FOREWORD BY *Tom Goldtooth*

University of Nevada Press Reno & Las Vegas

University of Nevada Press, Reno, Nevada 89557 USA
www.unpress.nevada.edu
Copyright © 2009 by University of Nevada Press
All rights reserved
Manufactured in the United States of America
Design by Kathleen Szawiola

Library of Congress Cataloging-in-Publication Data
Harney, Corbin, 1920–2007.
The nature way / Corbin Harney, as told to and edited by Alex Purbrick ;
foreword by Tom Goldtooth.
p. cm.
Includes bibliographical references.
ISBN 978-0-87417-788-6 (pbk. : alk. paper)
1. Harney, Corbin, 1920–2007. 2. Shoshoni Indians—Biography.
3. Shoshoni Indians—Social life and customs. 4. Shoshoni Indians—
Religion. 5. Shoshoni Indians—Civil rights—History—20th century.
6. Healers—West (U.S.)—Biography. 7. Religious leaders—West (U.S.)
—Biography. 8. Political activists—United States—Biography.
9. Antinuclear movement—History—20th century. 10. Nevada
Test Site (Nev.)—History—20th century.
I. Purbrick, Alex, 1973– II. Title.
E99.S4H269 2009
978.004'974574—dc22   2009015668

FRONTISPIECE: Corin Harney.
Photography by Thomas Gugler

This book has been reproduced as a digital reprint.

Contents

Foreword by Tom Goldtooth   vii

Preface by Alex Purbrick   xi

PART I   **My Own Story**

1 My Early Years   3
2 Working for My People   19

PART II   **Temme Nanewenee Sogobia
(Our Ancestors' Land)**

3 Mistreatment of the Native People   31
4 Travels Across Newe Land   41

PART III   **Newe Wisdom**

5 Healing with Our Prayers   55
6 Surviving on Nature's Medicine   65
7 The Nature Way   80

PART IV   **Surviving in the Modern World**

8 Protecting Nature   101

Notes   111

Foreword
by Tom Goldtooth

Corbin Harney was a Western Shoshone elder and spiritual leader working to protect the sacredness of our Mother Earth. In 1995 Corbin Harney wrote his first book, *The Way It Is: One Water, One Air, One Mother Earth*. This book introduced Corbin Harney to the world, as well as the struggle of the Western Shoshone to protect and heal their traditional lands from radioactive colonialism and the strength of the way of prayer.

In this second book, Harney draws further lessons and teachings he has gained from his work and relationships with many people around the world and from the wisdom and knowledge of his people, the Newe (Western Shoshone). This book opens the door wider for the world to gain a better understanding of the laws of Nature, how to work with Nature, and how to live in a Nature Way.

The Nature Way is a very timely book. More than ever before, life on this sacred Mother Earth is out of balance. Throughout the world, political, economic, environmental, social, and cultural pressures are rising.

Unsustainable development is being fed, like a hungry beast, by neocolonialism, capitalism, privatization, and globalization. The source of these pressures can be traced to the historical processes by which all humans have become increasingly alienated from the sacred Mother Earth. This includes alienation from self, community, and Nature. The long history of colonialism in the Americas seems to be threatened by cultures that have strong spiritual relationships to Mother Earth. This alienation has its roots in imperialism and colonialism, which have no ties to Nature. Intellectually, it is rooted in the Western concept of dualism, which sets humanity apart from Nature and legitimizes the view that humanity has not only the right, but also the obligation to subdue Nature for its own benefit. It is rooted in the institution of money, which creates a powerful illusion that people can live apart from, and are no longer dependent upon, Nature.

Indigenous peoples, in the Americas and globally, continue to be confronted by many threats to the environment. Traditional homelands of Indigenous peoples hold natural resources that the industrialized world covets: minerals, oil, gas, water, and timber. We hold "open" space where municipal, industrial, federal, and military toxic and radioactive waste is dumped, burned, stored, or reprocessed. Tribal nations from the Newe Sogobia to the villages of Alaska are experiencing high health risks from decades of radioactive and toxic exposure, most as a result of the military and the petroleum industry. Within the past ten years, evidence has emerged that toxic chemicals in the ecosystem and in human bodies disproportionately affect Indigenous peoples. These chemicals bioaccumulate and biomagnify in plants, soil, animals, birds, fish, and the food chain of both processed foods and other Indigenous traditional food systems. Food security is becoming an issue not just for Indigenous peoples, but for all humans and all life-forms.

Society's lack of environmental concern disrupts the ability of Indigenous peoples to protect their traditional territories. Indigenous communities are finding it difficult to maintain sustainable economic systems, to practice their traditional ceremonies, and to practice our hunting, farming, gathering, and fishing cultures. These cultures have been refined for millennia and have provided a way for Indigenous communities to flourish and live in a Nature Way. Language, prayers, and songs are the foundation of Indigenous identity both with the natural world and with each other. When the connection to healthy and sustainable ecosystems is disturbed by loss of habitat, biodiversity, and traditional food systems, the ability to pass on language and song closely linked with the natural world is disrupted as well.

Indigenous peoples of the United States and throughout the Americas hold valuable land and water resources that have long been exploited by the state and federal governments and by corporations trying to meet the high-consumption energy needs of an addicted industrialized world. Indigenous peoples have disproportionately suffered from the production and use of energy resources—coal and coal-bed methane mining, uranium mining, oil and gas extraction, nuclear-power and hydropower development—yet are among those who benefit least from these energy developments.

Indigenous peoples face inequity over the control of, and access to, sustainable energy and energy services. Territories where Indigenous peoples live are resource rich and serve as the base from which governments and corporations extract wealth, yet they are areas where the most severe expressions of poverty exist.

The sharing of traditional teachings from elder spiritual leaders such as Corbin Harney helps shape our work within the Indigenous Environmental Network, allowing us to maintain a perspective upholding the sacredness of life. We have opposed the sale and commodification of sacred medicinal plants used traditionally by our peoples by biological resource brokers, biopirates, and pharmaceutical companies. We are concerned about the market-based climate change solutions that privatize, sell, and trade the air with carbon-trading mechanisms between industry and governments. We have continued to assert and defend Indigenous human rights, cultures, land and water rights, and jurisdiction over resources and environment. We have also worked to present the traditional Indigenous perspectives on these issues for the well-being of all peoples and of the natural world. Living things are not held as property. Our Mother Earth and our plant and animal relatives are respected sovereign living beings with rights of their own.

Our Creator gave Indigenous peoples the responsibility to protect the land and natural life upon which our survival depends. Our sacred responsibility is to safeguard and protect this world. Human beings are not separate from the rest of the natural world, but were created to live in an integral relationship with it.

Mother Earth is sacred and must be honored, protected, and loved. This particular relationship has allowed us to conserve biodiversity for the survival of present and future generations. Our territories are natural, spiritual assets and are the fundamental basis for our physical and cultural existence. In our territories, we establish and maintain a deeply profound and sacred relationship with Mother Earth.

Understanding these Indigenous principles provides understanding and love for Mother Earth, Father Sky, and all creation and compassion for each other as human beings. All people must come to reidentify and realize their relationship with the sacredness of our Mother Earth and Father Sky. This will help us understand what our relationship is to the sacred female creative principle of Mother Earth.

It is a gift for humanity that Corbin Harney shares in *The Nature Way* as he recounts the beauty of his culture and the importance that Indigenous knowledge has to the survival of our Mother Earth. I consider Corbin's story as *teachings* that are cultural treasures of accumulated knowledge being passed on by an elder. These teachings within *The Nature Way* must be told to every human throughout the world. It is essential for the survival of all life-forms and for the future generations of all peoples throughout Mother Earth.

Mitakuye Owasin (All My Relations).

Tom "Mato Awayankapi (The Bears Look Over Me)" Goldtooth is Dine' and hunka Bdewakantonwan Dakota, from Minnesota. He is the executive director of ien, the Indigenous Environmental Network, an alliance of grassroots Indigenous peoples and communities working to protect the sacredness of Mother Earth and to address environmental and economic justice issues.

Preface

by Alex Purbrick

I first met Corbin Harney in January 2000 when I visited his healing center, Poo-Ha-Bah, in Tecopa, California, as a work volunteer. I had heard nothing of Corbin before other than what a friend had told me: that he was an elder and spiritual leader of the Western Shoshone, or Newe (which, literally translated, means "The People"), and was recognized as an international figure in the global antinuclear movement.

The Western Shoshone are the western band of the Shoshone tribe, whose homeland spans five states—Nevada, Utah, Idaho, California, and Montana. The Western Shoshone call their home Newe Sogobia (The People's Land) because traditionally there were no territorial boundaries and they did not claim to own the land or to call themselves anything other than "The People."

When I met Corbin, I only stayed at Poo-Ha-Bah for a few days because I had to return home to Europe. But fascination with the beautiful Mojave Desert and interest in Corbin's work and the projects at Poo-Ha-Bah lured me to return to America later in the year. It was at this point that Corbin talked to me about an idea he had to write a book about Nature and the stories of the Newe. I naively offered to help him with this project, and I say "naively" because I had never written a book before nor undertaken a project as huge as this. However, Corbin seemed to have faith in me and reassured me that it wouldn't be too difficult a job. Now, after working on this book for eight years, I know that writing a book can be more complicated than it first appears.

Corbin knew exactly the subjects and places he wanted to talk about, so in late summer 2000 we set off in his old camper van, following the tracks of thousands of generations of his ancestors across Nevada, southern Idaho, southern Utah, and California. Our travels ranged from sacred sites, old campsites, and hot, healing mineral waters to land devastated by nuclear testing. Everywhere we traveled, I photographed the things Corbin talked about and showed me, such as rocks, plants, mineral springs, and cave petroglyphs, so that we could refer to them as we developed the book.

It wasn't until we returned to Poo-Ha-Bah in the winter that Corbin had the chance to study all the photographs from our travels. Sitting in his trailer home in Tecopa, I recorded on tape his stories about all the various sites and subjects we had seen. Corbin had such a clear image in his mind of what he wanted to say in his book that I rarely had to ask him any questions or remind him of places we had been. I simply pressed Play on the tape recorder and listened to Corbin's voice until the tape ran out.

We didn't record every day, because Corbin had other commitments, whether it was his healing work at Poo-Ha-Bah or giving a talk at events throughout the southwestern states. By spring 2001, I had started to transcribe Corbin's recordings and rearrange everything into sections so that his thoughts would flow in an orderly sequence. I tried as best I could to keep the essence of his stories in the editing process to enable his voice to be "heard" throughout the book, with most accounts being word for word as they were recorded. However, some editing was required, because some sentences weren't as clear in print as they were when he spoke them.

Once I had completed several drafts of the manuscript, I told Corbin the section headings and showed him how I had put the stories together. He seemed content with the book at this stage, but we still had the task of finding a suitable publisher.

When I left the United States in 2004, I became somewhat despondent about how I was ever going to keep my promise to Corbin to get the book published. Fortunately, in March 2006 a good friend of Corbin's, Dixie van der Kamp, offered to help. Before she even approached a publisher, she printed out a copy of the manuscript for Corbin to read to ensure that he agreed with the final draft of the manuscript, that it contained everything he wanted to speak about, and that it was set down in a manner he approved of. Corbin said he wanted to read the text by himself, from beginning to end, and didn't want anyone else to read it to him. In November 2006, Dixie and her family visited Corbin at Poo-Ha-Bah. During their stay, Dixie talked to Corbin about the manuscript and asked him if he was happy with it. He said he had finished reading through the manuscript himself and had asked his caregiver to reread certain sections to him. He seemed enthusiastic about the work and thought it was "real good." Dixie asked him if he wanted to make any corrections or changes now that he had seen the final draft. As he looked through the manuscript, he made further comments about the importance of certain subjects such as the plants the Newe used for medicine, the various sites where Shoshone people had been massacred, and some of the places he had visited during his world travels. I have added his comments on these topics to the main body of the text where appropriate or have inserted his quoted revisions in a footnote in the section relevant to the subject. Some of Corbin's comments concerned topics he had already spoken about in the manuscript, so I did not feel it was relevant to repeat the information.

Corbin's emphasis on the plants and roots that he and his people relied upon for medicine illustrates how much he depended on the natural world for survival as well as in his work as a healer. In our modern world, many people cannot understand or believe that Nature has the power to cure sickness and disease through our use of plants, animals, water, and rocks, but the Newe depended on them to survive. They had no hospitals and pills; Nature was their doctor.

The Newe and all Native peoples, through their stories and beliefs, have their own form of natural science. Their view of the world and of life is based on what their ancestors have seen, heard, and experienced through dreams, visions, and ceremonies. Medicine people like Corbin can see and journey beyond the veils of different realms, where spirits and other beings coexist with our world. Modern science cannot yet explain the existence of spirits and paranormal events, yet to Native people they are all part of the mystery of life. Native people believe that we must include these spirits and other beings in our prayers and thoughts in order to keep balance on this Earth.

The devastating effect that nuclear energy has had and is continuing to have on our Earth is a message Corbin wanted this book to illustrate. Through all of his stories he talks about the importance of Nature in our lives to remind us how far removed we are from a natural way of living on the Earth. His stories do not follow any sort of chronological order. It is almost impossible to translate an oral culture such as Corbin's into written form in this manner. Corbin told me many stories that had no beginning and no end—one story simply seemed to continue into another. And this is the beauty of an oral culture. Time has no beginning or end. The stories wrap around each other in one big circle until you realize the story begins again, maybe slightly differently from before but still recognizable.

Another aspect of Corbin's oral culture is the use of his Idaho/Nevada dialect of Western Shoshone for the various plants and animals he mentions in the book. These have been written in italics; because the Shoshone language is not a written language, all words are spelled phonetically and may not be exact spellings. I thought it important to include Shoshone words, because Corbin used them in his stories and his descriptions of everyday life. English was not Corbin's first language, although he spoke it fluently.

This was one of the most powerful traits of Corbin's character. For a man who did not hold English as his mother tongue to become a spokesman on the global antinuclear stage is a remarkable achievement. But Corbin became an international personality quite by accident. Throughout his entire adult life, he campaigned tirelessly on behalf of his people for recognition of Western Shoshone land rights. Besides his role in organizing spiritual gatherings throughout Nevada in the 1970s, Corbin was known mainly to the Shoshone as a healer and a spiritual person. To white culture he was unknown during these years, and it was not until the Nevada Test Site demonstrations in the 1980s that Corbin became acknowledged as a spiritual leader for both the Shoshone and non-Native antinuclear protestors.

Corbin's prayers and inspiring words to all those attending the antinuclear protests at the Nevada Test Site (which is situated on Western Shoshone territory under an 1863 treaty with the U.S. government) achieved worldwide recognition and highlighted the fact that the government has conducted so many nuclear tests at the Test Site that this Western Shoshone desert homeland is now one of the most bombed regions on Earth. As a leading spokesman for the Shoshone, Corbin traveled around the world, speaking about nuclear and environmental problems in many countries. He addressed the United Nations in Geneva, Switzerland. He spoke against the horrors of nuclear radiation in Hiroshima, Japan. He was invited to Kazakhstan to heal their victims of radiation poisoning. While there in 1990, he formed the Nevada-Semipalatinsk Movement, an alliance between two Indigenous groups, the Western Shoshone and the Kazakh, who have both been affected by nuclear testing on their ancestral lands. He was called to Puerto Rico, Taiwan, and Hawai'i to aid Indigenous peoples there with their own environmental reclamation.

Some people may find environmental and nuclear issues too depressing or apocalyptic. But the beauty in Corbin's words lies in the fact that he offered solutions to these problems based on the everyday element surrounding his culture and all Indigenous peoples. This quite simply is the power of prayer: recognizing that everything on this Earth, ranging from plants and animals to rocks, water, wind, and even darkness, has a voice and spirit. If we do not talk and sing to them, they will die. To the thousands of non-Native protestors at the Nevada Test Site demonstrations, these simple words of wisdom struck a chord in many people's hearts and resulted in Corbin's becoming not only an environmental spokesman, but a man to whom people from all backgrounds and faiths could look for spiritual guidance and leadership. His philosophy that we are "one people on one

Mother Earth" created a bridge between Native and non-Native people as his words illustrated that radiation cancer affects all colors, all ages, all cultures, rich and poor.

Corbin's involvement with non-Native activists at the Nevada Test Site demonstrations enabled him in 1994 to form the Shundahai Network (*shundahai* is a Newe word that means "peace and harmony with all creation"). An antinuclear organization dedicated to raising awareness of nuclear issues and Indigenous sovereignty rights, the Shundahai Network arranged for Corbin to participate in numerous TV and radio talk shows throughout the United States, as well as being a keynote speaker at international conferences such as the Atomic and Hydrogen Bomb Conference in 2001 in Nagasaki, Japan.

Corbin never seemed to tire of traveling and spent most of his time giving talks to elementary, high-school, and college students, speaking at county fairs and music festivals, and defending Shoshone land rights to politicians and DOE (Department of Energy) officials at public meetings. As a result of his dedication to spreading awareness of the dangers of nuclear power and his commitment to encouraging peace and harmony on our Earth, Corbin received the Gandhi Peace Award in 2002, an annual prize bestowed by the Religious Society of Friends. He also received the International Nuclear Free Future Award in 2003 for his devotion to saving his land and the planet from the dangers of nuclear energy.

Corbin was also known as one of the few remaining Shoshone elders who was able to work with plants, animals, and spirits within Nature in order to help heal the vast numbers of people who asked for his help in curing their illnesses. He never charged for his healing work; instead, he believed that Nature had given him a gift to heal sickness, so it was his duty to pray for those who asked for help.

In his later years, it became harder for Corbin to constantly travel to those who were sick hundreds of miles away. He had a vision of a center where all people could come to receive traditional healing free of charge. In 1998 he established Poo-Ha-Bah, a healing center in Tecopa, southern California, which is centered around hot mineral springs. Corbin felt that the spirit of the water was strong in Tecopa and could promote healing. The name Poo-Ha-Bah (meaning "Doctor Water") came from Corbin's wisdom and prayers, as well as referring to his desert home, a place where he could relax and spend some time in relative peace and quiet.

I found myself constantly amazed at Corbin's extensive energy and untiring stamina as he spent each day from sunrise to sunset working selflessly to conserve all life on this Earth. His message that "we are all one people on one Mother Earth" is a vision we must all adhere to if we are to find peace in our world. However, he used to say many times that this was a belief that he had only realized in his elder years. When he was a young man, he hated white people because of the way they had treated his ancestors. He often said that when he was working as a cowboy he would rather fight a white man than work with him. He recounted many stories of his people's being mistreated by white people and always said that the white Europeans had no feelings when they came over to America. He could not understand why they had committed so many atrocities toward Native people over several hundred years.

The four years I worked with Corbin on this book were precious to me, as I gained insight not only into the life of an incredibly interesting and wise man, but also into the importance of Nature and this Mother Earth to our existence. As I lived and worked with Corbin at Poo-Ha-Bah for those four years, I helped arrange his public speaking engagements and generally became his personal secretary. He became a good friend to me, whose company I must admit I now miss dearly.

I have since returned to live in the windy, wet Shetland Islands in northern Europe, a far cry from the dry, dusty Mojave Desert. But part of my spirit will always remain in Newe Sogobia, and the memories of my time with Corbin I will treasure for eternity.

Since my writing this book, Corbin was diagnosed with cancer in 2006 and died on July 10, 2007, in Santa Rosa, California. Before his passing, he told his friends to remember that "we are one people. We cannot separate ourselves now. There are many good things to be done for our people and for the world. It is important to let things be good. And it is important to teach the younger generation so that things are not lost."

I feel sad that I did not get the chance to see Corbin before he passed—distance kept us from seeing each other again after I left America. But I feel the strength and beauty of his spirit and know that even in death his words, songs, and wisdom will grow more powerful as each season passes. Corbin planted a seed here on this Mother Earth, a seed of hope and a reminder that Nature will prevail, whatever the course humankind decides to follow. The younger generation are our future. I hope that this book will inspire and educate you, your children, and your grandchildren so that the light Corbin kindled for us will remain a beacon of wisdom to guide us back to the path of the Nature Way.

PART I

My Own Story

1 | My Early Years

My name is Corbin Harney, I'm a Shoshone Indian, what we call ourselves is Newe. I was born March 24, 1920, at Little Valley, Idaho [near the settlement of Bruneau, southern Idaho]. My mother passed on when I was two hours old, I've been told. She didn't have a white man name at all until the Bureau of Indian Affairs gave her a name, calling her Irene. She went by the name Irene Harney, but my grandma and the people that knew her from a long time ago remember her name was Shoshone. She didn't have a last name, because at that time the Indians throughout the country didn't have any fancy European names at all. They went by whatever name the midwife gave them, by what they looked like, how they acted, and so on.

Today I still don't know where my mother's resting place is. I have asked many people, trying to locate where she is resting, but nobody seemed to know. Some people have told me her resting place is in Duck Valley, Idaho, on the Idaho side of the border on Owyhee Indian Reservation in what they call Blue Creek, a little tiny knoll on the hill. But I have looked for her resting place and could never locate it.

How I began a life, my grandma and my grandpa took me with them, as I've been told. They took my mother's remains after she passed on, on a wagon from Little Valley to Duck Valley.

Going on a wagon took a few days, maybe it took two days to travel eighty miles. On the way we camped here and camped there.

I was always reminded that my mother is with me, as I was told later when I was old enough to hear what my grandma used to say.

At that time, when they buried her and put her in her resting place, my grandma and grandpa decided to go to Weezer, Idaho. This is where they came from. They're Shoshone from Weezer, Idaho. My grandma's name was Martha Washington, and her husband was Sam Harney. He was not my mother's dad but her stepdad.

My dad was killed before I was born, hunted down by the cavalry, as I was told by my grandma.

At my time, if you were richly, well-to-do, you lived in a tent, but if you were poor, like my grandma and my grandpa, we lived in a cellar, a hole in the ground in other words. This was the reason why we lived poorly. We didn't have too much to eat.

When I became old enough to chop wood and carry water, I remember I used to go out and chop sagebrush the best way I could, because my grandparents both were sick at one time. We were living away from some of the other Native people at that time.

So when my grandma said, "better go out and get some firewood," then I went out and collected some. I got little branches because I couldn't handle an ax. I did it the best way I could.

I remember when she used to make bread on a little tiny stove on an open flame. Then she'd make gravy. That's what we had every morning for breakfast, bread and gravy. We also used to have what we called salt pork. She used to fry that in the water, throw the water out, and then fry it again.

Of course they drank coffee, but at that time I didn't drink coffee. Before they became sick we used to go out and hunt for anthills, a lot of ants that's black and red. We call them *whorneetha*. In March, when it's cool in the mornings, I remember we went out to the anthills and took the eggs, little white eggs that looked like white rice. She used to put them in a cloth and squeeze them. Liquid like a milk comes out of the ant eggs, and my grandma used to fix that with water and I'd drink that milk. It was pretty rich stuff. At that time the ant eggs were used for many different things. They used to give them to babies, even if their mother was nursing them. Ant milk is called *annee am bechee* and is something my people used to feed me because at that time, when I was young, people were poor, they didn't have cattle, they only had horses. Very few people had cows. Black and red ants are something that my people used for making gravy. You don't see them anymore, but at that time there used to be a lot of them throughout the country. When they made gravy out of them, they just used the hind end, in other words the black part of it. They'd do away with the red part, the front part of the ant. I think all the Native people throughout the country used ant because ant gravy was sweet especially in February and March. Anytime after that or before that, the ant is sour. I remember a lot of people used to use ant eggs for fishing, to bring the fish onto shore. The ant eggs are important for a lot of different things. They've got a lot of grease. People used it in their hair, on their face, and on their body because it's got something in it that heals your skin. If you use ant milk on yourself, rub it on yourself, you won't have pimples on your body, because if you let that dry on you and keep it dry for one day, then it will heal your body.

It opens up your pores just like mud and then your body will breathe. Same with eating ant gravy, it gives your body a good digestive system.

What My Grandma Taught Me

I remember when she used to tell me stories about what they've been through. I remember when she used to tell me, "make sure when you're grown up, remember all the life out there that we're all connected to. Make sure when you get wood or whatever you collect, make sure you tell that brush or wood why you're taking its life. Make sure you go out there and talk to them and tell them why I need you. I need to warm my body with you and cook my food and warm the house where I live."

She explained to me that the sagebrush burning in the little tiny stove of ours, it had roots in the Earth, it can talk like we do, it thinks like we do, and it drinks a lot of water like we do. It takes in the sunshine, it takes in the wind and eats food. Those are the reasons why I have to say a few words to that sagebrush or whatever kind of wood there was and tell it the reasons why I want heat from it, because all the living things rely on water. If there was no water, we wouldn't have no flame at all, she used to tell me. It was hard for me to believe because a flame, I thought, came from dry wood. She said no, it didn't, it's got water in it.

That's the reason why it moves, it's got a spirit in it. Everything has spirit in it, she used to say. A lot of things she told me at that time it was hard for me to believe. When I grew older, then I began to realize how important it was for her to be saying those things. She used to tell me, "someday, when you get older, if you don't take care of what's out there, like all the living things, you're going to wake up and they're not going to be there. If they're not there, you're not going to survive. You cannot survive without them, they cannot survive without you. So we're all connected together as a life on this planet of ours."

She used to tell me, "don't destroy your Mother, because you've only got one Mother, we've all got that Mother. The trees have got that Mother, the animals, the berries, the roots, the birds all have the same Mother. This Mother of ours takes care of us if we ask our Mother to provide us with all the goodies. If we don't, we're going to miss those things someday."

Those are the reasons why, when I grew older, I began to look around me and began to realize how important those messages, those stories were.

She used to explain to me how important water is. We can make a lot of things out of that water. We can make coffee out of it, you can drink it. When I was young, I used to put sugar on dried up bread, stick it in the water and eat it. That's how I remember how sweet it was at that time, sweet bread, good water. She used to say that water's got life just like you do, don't harm it, don't throw anything in it, always take care of it.

"The trees," she said, "you cannot cut down for no reason. You have to talk to it first and explain why you're taking the tree down and taking the life of that tree. It's got a life like we do."

The European people came into this part of the country, and they cut trees down and made paper out of them. She used to tell me that the trees were all puzzled because they never told the trees what they were going to use it for and why they're making paper out of it. And today the tree is puzzled, the paper is puzzled. Those are the reasons why the paper today don't have no truth to it, it can keep changing. She used to tell me those things, which were true. I don't care what good words we put on a piece of paper, it'll turn on you. I remember one time people came to see my grandma with a stack of paper. They told her, she should go to their Sunday gathering in church. But she told them no, she wasn't, because she had her own beliefs and wasn't going to fall into their way of life. She said she was going to continue to follow the Nature Way of Life.

Power of Trees

She tried to explain to me, one tree out of a bunch might be a gifted tree. That gifted tree, you should really talk to in order for that tree to give you energy, and today throughout the world I see that. On one tree, maybe an animal would rub on it and sit under it. That one tree they pick out of a few trees, because that's their teacher or that's the one that gives them energy or that's the one that takes the sickness away from them. She used to tell me about willows, like making a baby cradle out of willow, for example. When the mommy was out gathering roots, doing her work, the baby is wrapped up in the baby cradle and hung on a tree. That tree occupies the baby by talking to it and singing to it, so the baby doesn't cry because the mommy isn't there. Then the mommy feeds the baby, hangs it in the shade, and that's where it spends its time, being kept happy by the tree. We enjoy the sound of a tree because when the wind comes through there, the tree is a filter for our air. When it comes through there, it's got a beautiful song, beautiful words. Our trees, which are supposed to be connected to us, are drying out.

They've got weak roots. You can't leave a baby on a tree nowadays, because it doesn't have a voice. The only time it's going to have a voice is if we pray to it, make sure it continues to have a voice and a song.

Snow/Duckavi

Snow comes down and covers the Earth. So underneath this snow, all the leaves under there, they get damp, they stay there all winter long.

In the spring of the year, when the grass begins to come up through the leaves, it makes a healthy covering for all the living things. The very first thing she used to tell me we do in the spring of the year, February/March, we had to pray for the snow. The snow has got a bug living inside it. Maybe you never seen it, or maybe you weren't paying attention when you were told about those things. The flea is purple in color, and in February/March, when you pick the snow up there'll be a lot of bugs in it. That's the one the people talked to and had their ceremonies for. Out of that snow comes more moisture, because those little tiny bugs, they're the ones that make water, my grandma used to tell me. It's not the snow. If you don't do those things, she used to tell me, your snow is going to be dry, it's not going to amount to anything. I don't care how much it snows, she used to say. Those are the reasons why we had ceremony for snow in February/March. Those were the beginning of our ceremonies.

We've got four ceremonies that we do. In April we have a ceremony to bring the moisture from above. The water has to be talked to, the clouds have to be talked to. They have to be thanked to bring the moisture down from above to wet everything down. If we don't do those things, she used to say, water's going to come down in a huge lump in one place that's going to wash away everything and take your soil from the hill and down here onto the flat. It's not going to rain in a circle for two to three days at a time and sprinkle rain, it's going to be in streaks. It's going to go one way, then it's going to change and do it different ways. Some places the rain is not going to be helping the Earth at all, she used to say.

Those are the reasons why we continued to have a strong connection together at one time.

The trees, the water, the rocks, all the living things are connected. We were connected to all of this at one time. When my grandma used to tell me the Mother Earth someday is not going to produce anything, so far I have seen that happening throughout the world. Today we're using different kinds of fertilizer that are getting stronger and stronger and stronger. What is it doing to our Mother soil? When we kill the Mother soil, the spirit of it, what do we do then? We're not going to be able to grow anything, we have already begun to see that.

Don't misuse a life of all different kinds, she used to say. Don't think for a minute your life is better than something else's life. Your life is the same as the tree, the rocks, or any animal life, bird life, and so on.

We have to take care of them because they were put here with us, so we are connected to them as we are connected to our Mother, our Father. They might be a little different from us, maybe they've got wings that can fly, but we are flying just like they are with an iron bird. But she used to talk about the iron bird. Someday that iron bird's going to be coming down, because the air that they fly in is not going to be there. Around us today, up above us, whatever we've done on this Earth, we're ruining something that's holding this Mother Earth in place. If we continue to do this, this Mother Earth of ours is not going to survive at all, because it's already begun to change. The Earth's going to be going in a different direction, the weather's not going to be perfect anymore, nothing's going to grow on this Earth pretty soon if you don't take care of it, she used to tell me. If you take care of different things, then they can work with you. She had a lot of things to tell me, but when I was young I didn't pay too much attention because I didn't know and maybe I didn't want to know. But as I grew older, I began to realize what she told me was very true.

My grandparents died a day and a half apart. I know they died in 1927, either in the last part of November or the first part of December. When they died, they left me with nothing and nobody but my uncle. His name was John Adam. When my grandparents both died, he was called to Fort Hall, Idaho, from where he lived in Duck Valley, Nevada. So he went down there to see his mother and his stepdad. When he was down there, at the same time his wife and their little baby died together. Before he even put his mother and stepdad away, I remember he told me, "you stay with these people here until I can get my things straightened out. I'm going back to Owyhee."

So he had to turn around and go back to Duck Valley. Then I was left there with a family who I really didn't know, but I stayed with them for a short time. That was during the fall of the year as I remember. I don't know how long I lived with them. I remember during that fall, when they were putting in winter wheat, I used to go out with this man harrowing the land, disking it, plaining it, and putting the seed in. I remember I used to lead his horses, two big Belgian horses, workhorses. I couldn't even reach their belly, I used to walk underneath them. They must have liked me, because they never bothered to even move when I walked underneath them and I'd touch them here and there. One time this family went to Blackfoot, Idaho, to get some groceries.

So that afternoon I was there at the house alone and I was told not to mess around with the latches on the door, but I guess when you're young you like to see what can happen. So I put the latches down on the door by mistake and the door slammed and I couldn't go back in the house. I didn't have nowhere to go, so that night I slept on top of those horses. They were eating out of a big trough, and I was trying to sleep on top of their backs because they were big enough to hold me. They never moved. They stood side by side, I guess, in case they thought if I fall I'll fall in between them. That's how smart those animals were. I remember when my grandma used to say, "an animal can save your life, they understand you, maybe you don't understand them but they understand you."

She used to tell stories about a lot of different things, about a bear or a wolf. They took care of young kids if they were lost, they'd take them to their den and raise them.

So those two horses did that to me, they made me realize what she used to say is very true. Those two horses saved my life from freezing 'cause I didn't have nowhere to get warm, but they kept me warm by me turning on them all night long. The next day, about noon, the buggy that the family traveled on didn't have anybody on it. They had a one-horse buggy. I unhooked this horse from the buggy, and I couldn't take the harness down because I was too small. So he had his head down, and I took the bridles off and gave him water and put him in the barn. Afterward the woman in the family came and asked me what I'd done, and she found out that I'd locked the house behind me, and she scolded me for it. She told me, "I told you not to mess around with that door." But what could I say?

Anyway I learned my lesson the hard way, that I'll never forget. That's how I came to understand about what my grandma used to say about a lot of different things.

Newe Pooha

And when I got a little bit older, my uncle was an Indian doctor or a *newe pooha,* as we used to call the medicine people. The white man called them witch doctors. He was a special healer for the Indian people. Shuka was his Indian name, the white man called him John Adam Washington. All my bloodline were healers. My grandma was a healer, I was told my mother was a healer. Our doctors were not ordinary people. They had to be given power by the Nature to work with certain kinds of spirits, of an animal, a bird, a stone, water, everything you can think of. They were healers because they were put here by Nature. It still goes on today. Some of the people today on this Earth of ours can still heal with their words, with their hands, whatever they use. Even some of the young people have still got powers. They can heal, but they have to have guidance from somebody telling them what they should continue to do.

Indian healers didn't go to school for it. They didn't just pick it up from somebody else, it was given to them by the Nature. Those were our doctors. Same with the animal life. Animals have their own healers. They heal each other, you can heal them, and they can heal you.

My uncle used to go around doctoring people when they were sick. Sometimes he doctored people all night long, singing songs and working on them. I remember I used to go with him because I didn't have anybody to stay with me at home. Then I began to realize as I grew older that I was one of those guys, one of those people that can see a sickness in a human. I never said anything to anybody, not even to my uncle, until one time we were coming home early in the morning after he had doctored this one guy, then I was telling him that I saw this kind of sickness in the guy that he was doctoring. He told me right then, "Don't tell me, keep it to yourself. Someday you're going to be doing the same thing as I'm doing, so don't mention it to me. If you see things, don't say anything about it."

So I began to realize that it's not for me to be telling people their sickness until I was asked to pray for them.

As I grew older I became ashamed of myself, because I used to remember the older people used to talk about how they were treated. What the white man did was to kill those kinds of people, because they thought they were witch doctors. I was scared and ashamed, so I never told anybody that I was one of those people.

One time, as I remember, when I was a young fellow, my uncle was doctoring this guy in the sweat lodge, and he got picked up by the Indian police and taken to jail. They left him there for two days, and this sick guy that he was doctoring kept asking for him. He wanted him to finish doctoring him. So the white-man doctor finally gave in and said, "Okay, if you want him to doctor you, you have to do it in the basement of the hospital, and I'm going to be there."

My uncle invited a few of the people that worked with him to sing songs with him. This old white-man doctor, he was sitting there watching what was going on. My uncle doctored this sick guy for two nights. On the third night, when this man became stronger, then this white-man doctor couldn't understand what he did to get him well.

Then another time after that, there was an Indian woman that was very sick that was in the hospital. This white-man doctor didn't know what to do for this woman. She was in the hospital dying, every day getting weaker and weaker. She kept telling the doctor, "I want Shuka to doctor me, I want to get out." Her family told the doctor, "We're going to get her out and get that Indian doctor to work on her."

Finally he gave in and said okay. Again he asked my uncle to doctor that woman in the basement. So he did, he doctored her in the basement. Within one week this woman got strong enough to walk out of that hospital, and from there on this white-man doctor became friendly with my uncle, told him what a wonderful thing he'd done, how did he do it?

He knew that my uncle didn't touch the woman at all. He just ran his hand over the top of her head and gave her a drink of water and sang songs and a lot of praying. What kind of medicine did he use?

My uncle told him it's the spirit that does the work, not him. All he is, is a translator for the spirit. The doctor became friendly after that. I remember, he used to ask my uncle to go to the hospital and pray for some of the people that were sick.

Running Away from School

When I was about nine years old, my uncle was told that I had to go to a Bureau of Indian Affairs (BIA) boarding school. If I didn't, the BIA were going to put him in jail. So he told me, "it's up to you, you're the one that's going to have to decide, because you lived without me for so long and now I've tried my best to keep you with me. I know school is not going to educate you. I know school is not going to do you no good, because you've got a mind of your own."

So I ran away from my uncle's home. I lived in the haystacks even during the winter months. I went up in the hills. I stayed up in the hills for many months, surviving off the land. This was important for me to learn the Nature Way of Life. The Nature is the one that taught me how to survive off the land. Some days I didn't have anything to eat. I had holes in my clothes. My shoes had holes in them. I used to go around picking up cardboard boxes and make soles out of them to go inside my shoe, but that didn't last in the winter weather, so I finally started cutting up inner tube and putting that around my shoe, which kept my shoes dry for a while. I had a coat that was ready to fall off, but I had to take care of it the best way I could. As far as eating, I used to make traps to catch cottontails. Maybe I'd have two meals a week. I was hungry, but I was scared at the same time in case I was sent away somewhere because my uncle used to tell me, "You're going to be sent away to some school, maybe back east somewhere." But I didn't want to go, I didn't want to leave. Those are the reasons why I had to run away from my uncle's house.

A fellow by the name of George Thomas took me in, bought me shoes, pants, shirt, and a brand new coat, and he told my uncle that he had done this for me. My uncle told him that he would pay half of what he had spent on me, and I guess he did. I stayed with him for about a week, and then I went off someplace else and somebody else would find me and take me to their home, which for most of the time were tents.

It was awful, the experience I went through. I got picked up one time by the BIA police. I was put in jail. From jail I was put in school for one week. On Monday the policeman took me to school and dropped me off in the school yard at nine o'clock in the morning. I didn't have anything to eat or drink, the only meal I had was lunchtime at the school. That went on for four days, and then Friday came. The policeman used to pick me up at four in the afternoon. Either he forgot or he was too busy. All the schoolchildren had left, and I was in the school yard by myself, and I thought that there was no use hanging around there, so I took off. I was found along the road a few miles out from Duck Valley Reservation in Nevada. I was picked up by Indian people and taken to Mountain Home in Idaho, where I stayed for a few days, and then from there back to Duck Valley again, and the people took care of me there for about three or four days. Then I left again, because I knew I was going to be picked up by the police or sent away somewhere. This time when I left I went further into Idaho. I got picked up again at a restaurant. The guy that picked me up took me to Twin Falls, Idaho, on Highway 30, as they used to call it at that time. This guy asked me if I was hungry, and I said, "yeah I'm hungry," so he said, "we'll stop at this restaurant and eat."

I guess at the same time he called somebody, and before I got through eating the police arrived. They dragged me out and took me to Twin Falls jail. The next day I was picked up by Indian police again and taken back to Duck Valley.

At that time I was put into the care of the superintendent of that reservation. He had two boys. He had a big house that he lived in, and he put me in the basement. It was nice and warm, because it had a big fire down there. I went to school with the two boys of his. They didn't like me, because I was wild and I didn't talk good English. But anyway they played with me. They didn't care. They used to push me around, and whatever I picked up, like the toys they played with, they used to take away from me or if I wanted it they'd throw it at me.

I was there for a week I guess, and then I was sent on a bus to the Stewart Indian School in Nevada, right out of Carson City.[1] The Stewart Indian School was established way back in 1890 by the Bureau of Indian Affairs to educate the "savage Indian," as they called it.

They had to educate them the European way. Most of the Indian kids that went to school there didn't understand any English, and they were punished for that. The European way was very hard to understand because it was something new to us, learning by the books. All we understand as Native people is how the Nature works. The Stewart Indian School was established to teach their way, so we would lose our ways and become one of them. But they didn't realize that we're part of this Earth. We work with the Nature. We didn't know a thing about books. They taught a totally different way of life. The way that they came here, trying to teach us their way, we couldn't adapt to that for many, many years. We still want to talk our Native tongue, live our

Native ways. They wanted us to get away from our "hard life," as they called it, but it wasn't hard. It was working with the Nature, learning how to stay healthy and strong. They changed us, and today those are the reasons why we're lost. We forgot our ways, we forgot our languages, we forgot our songs. And today we don't try to take care of each other because we're so jealous of one another. We have changed a lot. We started to not take care of what was put here by the Nature.

A lot of kids went to the Stewart Indian School. When I got there Friday evening, right away the matrons started scrubbing us with a big hand brush that they scrubbed the floor with. I remember one kid was crying. He had blood on his shoulder, they kept rubbing him because his skin was a little darker. I guess they were trying to make him white. I remember he used to cry and cry. He just couldn't help but cry. Most of the kids had their knees and elbows scrubbed until they got bloody. I didn't like that at all. I remember they used to scrub me. I'd try my best not to holler or cry, but it hurt. I remember thinking to myself, if I cry, they're going to get worse, so I had to be strong and stick it out the best way I could. I remember one boy that was lying next to me that cried all night long because he was so sore from bleeding, and the next day he got punished for getting the sheets all bloody. It wasn't his fault, but he suffered for it anyway. The girls were poked in the head with a sharp pencil, there'd be blood running down the side of their face. The boys, their ears were pulled and they were hit with a ruler between the head and the ear. The kids with long hair, their hair was clipped off and they were given clothes that were all the same, some of them white and some of them gray in color. This is when I decided it wasn't good for me because I'll never learn anything there, all I'm going to be is disgusted.

So I decided to leave because I didn't like the way they treated the kids. Sunday morning came and I decided to run away. I already had my mind made up that I was going to leave. At that time Stewart was about three miles away from Carson City. There was nothing between but tall sagebrush and a lot of lizards.

Working for My Living

So I headed out after breakfast. I stuck some biscuits and some boiled potatoes in my shirt and I went to Carson City, which at that time was about three miles from Stewart School. In Carson City at that time there was just a one-way street, and I got to the end of the street going toward Reno. A guy picked me up by the name of Dewey Sampson and took me to Reno. He asked me if I wanted to work for a little bit. He said some people in Nixon, Nevada, were putting up a diversion dam, and they needed a wrangler for their horses. There were quite a few people working there with around thirty to forty horses. I'd take these horses out on the hills in the morning and watch them and bring them back in the evening. Sometimes I had to bring horses in at noon, so the people that were working with their horses could change their team. That time I was paid one dollar a day. After that, I left Nixon and went back to Owyhee. When I arrived in Owyhee, I had to hide out because I didn't want to be picked up again by the law enforcement. I didn't want to be put into a BIA public school or a boarding school, so I worked for a cattle company. I didn't talk much English, but I worked for about six or seven buckaroos. I had my own set of horses.

I suffered from the beginning of my life, but after I began to work for the ranching company, I had a little money to buy myself clothes and food.

When I was working for the cattle company, I knew a guy who was a shovel operator. One time he asked me if I wanted to be his grease monkey. "If you are going to be my grease monkey," he said, "you can learn how to run a machine."

So I worked there for him, and during the early hours I would start the machine and grease it up. Then one Monday morning this operator didn't show up for work. There were eleven dump trucks that were building a road, putting gravel down, and the truck drivers asked me if I could load them up, and I said, "No, I can't because I don't know how."

So one guy that I knew and trusted that was always riding around with me on horses, he told me, "if you don't load me up I'm not going to get any money, but if you load me up then I can continue to draw my wages." I finally agreed to it. I said "okay, I'll do what I can."

So I loaded him up, another truck pulls in, I load him up, and one after another the trucks kept coming back. For about a week I guess I did that, and then the boss came and said, "you've been doing this for a few days already. If you want the job you can have it, since the operator didn't show up back to work." I told him, "no, I'll wait until the operator shows up, but I'll continue to work and load the people up with the work that they wanted to do."

This is how I started to learn how to work with machinery. I worked with all different kinds of machinery after that, from shovel to bulldozer, from bulldozer to scrapers, and this is where my beginnings as a machinery operator started. I got paid a little bit of money, better than the truck drivers. I think I got one dollar and ten cents a day and the truck drivers got one dollar a day.

2 | Working for My People

was drafted to the army in 1942 during the Second World War when I was twenty-two years old. They drafted anybody. Everybody and anybody! I saw people that were crippled that were drafted into the army at that time. I was only in there a very short time, because I didn't believe in going across the big water to go kill somebody—over what? They didn't do anything to us here, but our government wanted us to go over there and kill them because they were our enemies, we were told. But our land, our way of life was a little different in this part of the country. We were concerned about life, we had to take care of one another, we shared things together. This is why, when I was drafted into the army, I didn't appreciate it. They put me onto every kind of test they thought about, but I kept telling them, "I don't know!"

So they finally gave up on me because I didn't know how to do anything. Whatever they told me to do, I just couldn't do it. After a while they told me to dig a pipeline and ditches by hand with a pick and shovel. But I didn't know how to handle them. I had blisters in my right hand because my right arm was crippled.

I knew I had to do what I could to get out of the army. I prayed every day and night that I would get out of the army and return home. So I kept telling people that I didn't know how to do things. Within a very short time of six months, they gave me an honorable discharge. I got out of the army and I appreciated that, because I didn't believe in going across the sea to kill someone over there. That wasn't my idea.

Battle Mountain Gathering

I knew a guy called Jim Street from Fallon, Nevada. He was a friend of mine. He and I talked about a lot of different things, especially Indian problems. We thought that getting the Shoshone together would be the way to unify us as a people.

So Jim and I agreed to start a gathering in Battle Mountain, Nevada, in 1947. We asked people throughout the country to attend the gathering. The Battle Mountain business people appreciated the idea, and they donated food. One rancher donated a cow. The other ranchers donated different kinds of food. This is when we talked to Patrick McCarran, the senator for Nevada, about what we were organizing, and he thought we were doing something great for the Shoshone people. He even came out and told us that the state should really understand what the Shoshone people are doing, and that they should appreciate us bringing back our ceremonies. As the time went on, not only Jim Street and I were involved, but Doc Blossom, Walter Leech, and quite a few other people started to help in organizing the gathering. The town people got involved in our plans, as did the county commissioners who came out during the opening of our ceremonial grounds. Lincoln Ranching Company donated their field for us to hold the gathering.

A lot of official people came to the gathering. Both Patrick McCarran and Dan Shovelin were nominated as honorable members of the Battle Mountain Shoshone. Dan Shovelin was a businessman from Battle Mountain and had donated a lot of lumber for us to build our platform. He had also brought in a lot of non-Indians to the gathering.

We had ceremonies for four days, day and night. We did what our forefathers have done. We danced, we showed the non-Indians the different games that we played, like football and hand games.

Hand games were popular with the Shoshone people. People used to sit in two lines facing each other. There were two pieces made out of bone or wood. One of the pieces had a black stripe in the middle, whereas the other piece was plain. One person would hold these in their hand and the opposite side had to guess in which hand someone is holding the plain piece. Then they would win more points if they guessed right. The side with most points won the game.

We held another gathering the following year in 1948, but instead of holding it on the rancher's property, we held it on the Battle Mountain Indian colony. Then a sad thing happened at that time. Somebody got hit by a car and lost their life at the intersection. So we decided it wasn't the place to hold it. People appreciated the gathering, but we didn't like the idea of what happened so we never did it again.

Land Rights

In the 1950s and 1960s, some Shoshone people started to talk more about Western Shoshone land rights. I was involved in this for many years. I talked about how we, the Shoshone people, own land under the 1863 Ruby Valley Treaty of Peace and Friendship.

I also talked about the Tutuwa Treaty.[1] Some people say it's an agreement because it was never ratified as a treaty by the United States government. But I talked about it to the people, because Chief Tutuwa from Reece River near Austin, Nevada, made an agreement with the white man that the Indian people owned the land but that the white man could share it in a peaceful way.

This is the same as the Ruby Valley Treaty of 1863 in that the United States government did not keep their word of promise and honor Shoshone land rights. I traveled to different Shoshone reservations and powwows in the 1950s, 1960s, and 1970s talking about these things so the people would understand how important these treaties were.

As the years went by, then some of us Native people started to write letters to Congress, the Bureau of Indian Affairs, and the Department of the Interior. We chose Glen Holley from Battle Mountain as our leader. We tried to bring in funding in order that we could continue to travel throughout the country talking to people about the Ruby Valley Treaty. It was tough. In 1972, Glen Holley was contacted by Joel Freedman. We agreed to it that he was going to film our struggle. This is when the *Broken Treaty at Battle Mountain* film was made in 1974.[2] It was narrated by Robert Redford, and it showed many people the problems we were having and our work to promote the treaty.

A lot of our own people were divided on the issue of the treaty and land rights, because the Bureau of Indian Affairs wanted to pay the Shoshone $25 million for their land. Of course they didn't tell us right away that it was for the land. They told us it was for the damages that the European people had done to the land. After a while it changed, and they told us that they were going to give us money for the land and then they would keep the land. We started asking questions about those things. We even hired an attorney to look into it, but the attorney that we hired at that time talked good and gave a lot of promises, but in the end we didn't get any further than we had been before. From there on, little by little we began to lose our rights.

Treaty Days

Larry Piffero, Benson Gibson, Joe Prior, Frank Temoke, Felix Ike, and myself decided to organize a Treaty Days Gathering from October 1 to 3, 1988, so that people could gather together and recognize how important the treaty of Ruby Valley was to the Shoshone people.

We held a gathering out there at the David Neff Ranch in Ruby Valley, and the ranchers donated beef and other food. We talked about raising awareness of the Ruby Valley Treaty and why we should be bringing this to the attention of the United States government, especially Congress. We formed a Shoshone Elders Council to pass on Shoshone ways and language to the young people. The State of Nevada authorized us to have a Treaty Days at Ruby Valley and even gave us a seal that was a Proclamation by the Governor.[3]

We had Treaty Days for three years, and lots of people supported us, even the local ranchers. A lot of people came, a lot of people listened to what we had to say. We had our ceremonies, we talked to the young people, we played our traditional hand games. It was really important that something like this had to happen with a few of us getting together.

Spiritual Gatherings

For many years I organized spiritual gatherings, trying to teach our young people about living a spiritual way of life.

In the early 1970s there were three ladies, Dagmar Thorpe, Debbie Harry, and Pearl Dann that tried to start spiritual gatherings on different reservations and communities.[4] All the communities that they went to didn't want a spiritual gathering to be held at their community, because it would draw too many problems.

So they came to me one morning and asked me what I thought about a spiritual gathering. I told them it was very important, because that was what our forefathers have done long before. So they told me the story that they had been refused and asked me if I could take over and see if I could talk to the people in Owyhee. Owyhee is a big reservation for the Shoshone people, it's mixed with Paiutes also. I went to the Owyhee Tribal Council and asked them if we could use Skull Creek for our spiritual gathering. They said it sounded good. I started preparing for it, asking a few of the young people there if they could give me a lending hand. There were quite a few people at that time got together, and we held a spiritual gathering. Quite a few people came from throughout the country, from California, Oregon, Canada, Wyoming to name a few. I led the spiritual gathering. Of course I had the three ladies supporting what I was doing, and they were the ones that raised the money to set up the gathering. I think we had the gathering for four years at Skull Creek, then we moved it to Battle Mountain Indian Colony. We had it there for one year, but people didn't appreciate it, the young people didn't really understand what it was about.

We had a sweat lodge at Battle Mountain. We had a sweat there every Sunday, and this is when a lot of different people didn't know that I could pray for people until the time when one of our leaders passed out in the sweat lodge and my wife called me in. I went in there and doctored this person until she came back to consciousness, and the people in there saw what I had done. From there on I was recognized as one of their spiritual people, and I became the spiritual leader of the two ladies that I worked with, Florence and Eunice. They said for to me to lead them because I was a man.

Sun Dance

I have worked in many Sun Dances before. In the 1920s my uncle, John Adam, used to run Sun Dance in Fort Hall, Idaho, in what they call Bannock Creek. They had a Sun Dance out there for a few years, right across from a flour mill. This is how I knew about Sun Dance and what it was about. This is the reason why some people asked me if I could start a Sun Dance in Owyhee. This was in 1975. We gathered the young people together and said we were going to have a Sun Dance. Everyone appreciated it, everybody said it was a good idea.

Sun Dance is a very important part of our lives as Native people. This is where we get our strength. If you're a gifted person, if you're losing your strength, when you're in the Sun Dance you can pick up what you have lost or the power that you're losing. You already had the power to begin with, but you would start to lose it if you did not follow what the Nature has told you to do. A lot of things the Nature has told you to do, but maybe you don't want to do those things or maybe you're too lazy to do it.

This is where we can foresee why we were given that kind of power. This is Nature's gift. Sun Dance was set up so we could renew or repower ourselves. The healers ran the Sun Dances. They are the only ones that can guide a Sun Dance, because that's their gift from Nature.

We go into a Sun Dance for four days without drinking water and without eating. Each person runs back and forth to a cottonwood pole in the middle of the Sun Dance arbor as singers sing different songs. All the songs were connected to the pole, the arbor, the whistle, or a spirit. Each song meant something, so you as an individual had to really make up your mind to do what you could to help your people by renewing your power.

The men had their Sun Dance in one area, the women had their Sun Dance separately in a different area. Not just anybody could go into Sun Dance, you had to go through a Sun Dance leader. He is the one who chose you to be in the Sun Dance.

There were a lot of different ways of doing Sun Dance at that time but this was the Shoshone Sun Dance. The Shoshone don't pierce their bodies like some other tribes do.

In June 1941 there was a Sun Dance held in Wells, Nevada. It was held where the old Indian camp used to be, where the Pabawena family lived. It was run by two women, Eunice Silva and Florence Vega, and this is where I met them and I began to be acquainted with them.

The women's and men's Sun Dance were both alike in that they were pretty strict. Once you were in the arbor, you were in there until the end. You could not leave the arbor without a guide taking you to the restroom and bringing you back. They had to be with you all the time. On the morning of the fourth day, they came out of the arbor and were blessed by the Sun Dance leaders. The first thing they ate was a little slice of watermelon. After they ate the watermelon, then they gave them a little drink of water.

As time went on things changed, and now Sun Dance has both men and women dancing together and is not so strict.

A World Traveler

A guy called Bill Rosse one time asked me in 1985 if I would join him in getting the word out to the people about the nuclear testing at the Nevada Test Site. The Nevada Test Site was set aside for use as a military testing ground by President Truman in 1951. But the United States government never looked at the fact that this is Shoshone land under the Ruby Valley Treaty of 1863. We were told a lie. They said under that treaty that they were going to protect the land, not explode thousands of nuclear bombs on it. My people used to camp on that land before it was a test site. I didn't appreciate what the nuclear bombs were doing to the land, the animals, the birds, and the plants. They were put there by the Nature to survive off the land, but now they're all gone. The medicine roots of all different kinds that were put there by the Nature. Those things I have seen disappear from the Nevada Test Site.

Bill Rosse told me, "You're the man that doesn't have any responsibilities because your wife died in 1985, you don't have any children, so you should go out and talk to people around the country. We'll try to raise funding for you to travel."

So this is why I became a world traveler. I was invited to go to Japan to witness what we have done to the people there during the time when the United States dropped those two atom bombs on Hiroshima and Nagasaki. It was awful to see how many people suffered and got burned from the blast. I was told that when that bomb was dropped on Hiroshima, it landed in the middle of the town, next to the five rivers that flow through there. A lot of people had to run to the river because the radiation was so hot on their bodies, and they dived into the water. Many, many Japanese people died when we dropped the bomb on them, and many people were crippled.

When they dropped those bombs over there in Japan, they killed everything. Most of the people suffered, and today they're still suffering. This is something we should never forget that we have done to the Japanese people.

I was also invited by the Russian people to go to their country and talk to the people there about the nuclear testing the Shoshone people have seen on our land. They asked me to come to heal the radiation sickness.

When I went to Russia, I saw the same thing happening there that's happened here at the Nevada Test Site. The people are suffering, the people are complaining to their government. It was really dangerous in some areas like Chernobyl. The Russian people took me about seven miles away from it. It was so hot there, they didn't want me to go any closer than seven miles. I don't think anything survived when that meltdown at Chernobyl happened. Some of the people that lived near Chernobyl were crippled for life. They were beautiful people concerned about life just like us. I will never forget those things as long as I live.

I was asked to go to Puerto Rico and talk about nuclear power, because on the shoreline of Puerto Rico they've got a nuclear-power plant that sucks water from the ocean to cool down the reactors and pump it back into the ocean. I spoke to the people there and told them the problems that nuclear plant is going to create for them in their life. I talked about how important it is to have a beautiful land and a beautiful life, but their life is not beautiful because the United States is forcing them to take nuclear energy and nuclear weapons into their country. I have seen where the United States has a submarine base under a mountain in Puerto Rico. It's a huge tunnel going from the shore into the mountain. This is what they live with, and their government is telling them the same thing, how good it is that the submarine base is there to protect them, but it's not so.

All the creeks, all the water on the mountainside don't have any life in them at all. They protect the coffee there, but they're not protecting the fruit, like the bananas, oranges, grapefruits, and peaches, because they were told they had to protect the coffee beans. We went out gathering palm sap. There was a group sitting around, laughing and joking. I asked them if they had any songs for this. Only one old lady said, "By God, yes, we used to but we forgot." The more I talked to people, the more appreciation I got from each country. They all said the same thing, that they've been misused by their government. Our leaders are supposed to be listening to us, they even said so in the elections. They come around and tell you what they can do for you to make your life better than what it is. But I see that when they get to Washington, D.C., everything changes. I've been to Washington, D.C., I've talked to our senators about how concerned I am for the land, the animals, the birds, and all the creatures that were put here on this Earth with us.

Radiation is something that's really dangerous.

I always wanted to have a beautiful land, beautiful water, beautiful air, beautiful food for the younger generation so they can continue their life and enjoy each other and take care of each other instead of taking each other's life. This is why I have traveled all over the world talking about the importance of Nature and the land.

PART II

Temme Nanewenee Sogobia
(Our Ancestors' Land)

3 | Mistreatment of the Native People

We, the Indian people, were prisoners of war. We still are today throughout the country. The United States government has got a law against us in whatever we do. They took our rights away from us, they're still doing it today. Before the Europeans came into this country, we had the rights to do whatever. We could go fishing, we could go hunting, and we shared things together. Now we can't fish, we can't hunt, we can't do anything unless we are a member of a federally recognized tribe. What does that mean? They're controlling us, telling us what we can and can't do.

Not too long ago our people have been slaughtered by the thousands. Why? Because they're occupying the land that somebody else wants. Today, throughout the world it's that way. The Europeans say they discovered America. They didn't discover it. The Indian people were already here. This is their land, and today somebody else says it's their land. They didn't give them anything. They say they gave them money. They say they gave them a sack of flour or patted them on the back, telling them a lie by saying, "we're going to make a treaty with you people." The treaty was made and today they don't recognize the treaty.

And today the government says to the Native people throughout the country, "we have paid you for your rights and for your land." The government has given the Native people throughout the country only a very small amount of money for the land that they go on to sell for a few hundred times more than what they have given the Native people. They say the value of the land at that time was only so much, but they turned it around and sold it to each other when they don't even have a title to the land at all under their law. They're supposed to have a title to that land if they bought it from whomever. Where's their document that reads that they have bought it from an individual? Or are they just saying the law is on their side? There's no law on the Native side at all. Indian people became slaves for the European people when they first came. They worked for the white man. The white man had to write a check for the Indian people, but the Indians didn't have a European name so they couldn't write them a check. So the white man gave the Indians their own name. That's the reason why throughout the country the Indians are carrying European names. They worked for the white man because there wasn't any way that they could have continued to roam the country freely like they did before, because they were being hunted down.

Not too long ago I remember Indian women used to work for white folks, ironing and washing their clothes for a dollar a day. From dark to dark sometimes they had to work. This is how they worked with the white man, and this is how we started to learn their language.

This English language is a complicated language for us Indian people, but we had to learn. "Yes" and "no" were the first words I could say. I still don't understand everything, but sign language was very important at that time. The men did gardening for the white folks, they helped them in whatever help they needed. It was hard from the beginning, but as time went on it taught us a totally different way of life. We could buy things like a sack of flour, beans, maybe coffee. We didn't know anything about sacks of flour, because we used to make our flour out of roots or different kinds of herbs to make bread.

So this is something that my people have done, working for the white man, putting up their hay, working their cattle, training their horses. We have come a long way, and today we've got their language, we understand their ways, but they still won't let us give them an idea, we can't tell them what to do because we don't know anything in their eyes. For a few hundred years we were told, "you Indian people are savages, you don't know nothing, you're dumb, you're dumber than an animal." But today we all realize that an animal is not dumb. An animal is a smart creature. He still survives on this land.

My people, the Native people throughout the country, were hunted down by the cavalry and the miners. The War Department couldn't round up all the Indian people, so they turned to the miners and the fur trappers for help. They put a bounty on the Indian people's head. One hundred dollars for the scalp of a man, fifty dollars for a woman, and twenty-five dollars for anyone under eighteen.[1]

This is what took place at one time, our scalp was worth money. A lot of those people that hunted us made a lot of money turning our scalps in to the War Department.

When I went to the Smithsonian National Museum of Natural History in 1994, I saw many Indian scalps in their private storage collection.[2]

I remember seeing all of those iron pots in Fort Ruby, Ruby Valley, Nevada, where they used to boil my people. They're not there anymore. The cavalry would feed the bodies to the other prisoners and make them eat their own people. Iron lugs were put onto our ankles, huge balls of iron, so that we couldn't run away. In what they called a fort at that time, we were held captive like an animal. From there we were marched someplace else. We were herded like sheep under the guns of the government. If you didn't behave, then this is the time that they took your life.

My grandma used to tell me stories of when she was a little girl, how her and her mother were taken prisoner of war by the War Department. They were marched from Idaho all the way to Vancouver, B.C. The cavalry on horseback marched them and didn't give them anything to eat. Some of the young people and some of the old people couldn't make it, so their life was taken on the way. Babies in other words, when they cried because they were hungry, they were taken from their mommy. They were held prisoner for six years on the island there. They didn't have anything to eat. The only thing they could survive on was fish. I guess every now and then the War Department would come onto the island with their boats to bring a little food, but no medicine. During the winter months they had to huddle together to keep warm. During the night there was no wood of any kind. They had to drink the ocean water. They couldn't do anything. They were told to take care of themselves. I was told by my grandma that they had to eat raw fish. You see, the Indian people had a natural power to bring fish to the shore by singing to them and talking to them, because the animal life, the fish life had said to the people at one time, "I'm here for you. If you take care of me, I'll take care of you."

They had to struggle the best way they could. Many of the Indian folks that were held prisoner passed on. When they passed on, then the War Department threw them in the river so the fish could eat the human flesh.

According to my grandma, her mother put her on her back and came across from that island to the shoreline of Canada. How she did this, I was told, was because her mother used to have the power with water. She could walk on water. This is something nobody understood, how they got off that island. When they came back home to their stomping grounds, back to where they were at one time before they were captured, they found that the miners and settlers had taken their homes and land for their own.

Smokey Valley

In Smokey Valley, Nevada, there used to be a lake at one time, but it's not there anymore. All it is now is an alkali lake bed.

The War Department was gathering Shoshone people from Stoneburger Creek in Nevada to take them to camps where they held them prisoners of war. They chased an Indian family across the lake sixteen miles, down the flat, coming over this dry lake, which at that time had water in it. When the War Department came across the lake on their horses, they couldn't make it through the water, so they had to go south around the lake in order to get to where the Indian people were at. The Indian people knew where to cross, so they made it over to the other side much more quickly than the cavalry. The Indian people went up onto the white rimrocks across the valley from the lake and stayed up there for seven days. At that time the cavalry couldn't get at them. They surrounded the area, they got up on a higher ridge and tried to shoot across. The gunpowder they used was slugs, which didn't go too far, and they couldn't see them up there.

How did that family survive on that rock? It would be interesting to know how during the night the man went down someplace to get food and water. Somehow the War Department couldn't get to them for seven days. They finally gave up on them. They thought they were dead up there anyway, without no water, no food.

I think the War Department, at that time, wanted to eliminate the Indian people.

Let's Talk About the True History

When the Indian people were having a gathering, the Bureau of Indian Affairs police would come and pick them up and really work them over if they talked back to them. Our own people have been brainwashed by the Europeans to mistreat their own people. This is wrong. Some people were really mistreated, some people were treated good. It all depends on you, if you follow their way and be a puppet for them. I know many, many times the young people were taken away from their mother and father to change their way of life by putting them into Mormon schools. They were held prisoner by the Mormon Church many, many miles away from their reservation, away from their community, away from their people.

I went to Washington, D.C., in 1994 to bring back the remains of what the police of Humboldt County have done to one of my people.

His name was Shoshone Mike.[3] His family was massacred in 1911, near Kelly Creek Ranch in Nevada for reasons that somebody else told them, that they had killed a white man's cow, but the white man was the one that killed the cow and accused the Indian. So a sheriff's posse went after him and his family for many, many months trying to track them down. They could never get near them until they were hungry. Mike and his family didn't have much to eat, so they cornered them and massacred them.

I remember looking at their skulls in Washington, D.C., and asking the people, "are you proud of what they have done to the family of Shoshone Mike's, all eight of them?"

A little girl, three years old, was shot from the back of her head and her skull was all blown up. Each person had two bullet holes in their skull.

This is something that nobody wants to talk about, the true history. It is going to come out someday, the truth, and we're all going to know about it, because the Native people have suffered under the hands of our government. Not too long ago we, the Native people, were refused service in the restaurants. When we ordered our food, they fed us in the alleys. Not too long ago, we couldn't travel on a bus or on the railroad. At one time the railroad said to the Indian people, "we're going to put this railroad on your land and you can have a free ride back and forth." But when they decided no more riding on trains, then when you got on the train you were asked to either stand between the two cars or sit in only one area. Same with the bus. You sat in the back, you weren't allowed to sit close to a white man, because the white man was so clean whereas the Indian was dirty. He was a "savage," the white man said.

Treaty Rights

In Cherry Creek, out of Ely, Nevada, in what they call Ruby Valley, is where the treaty was signed between the United States government and the Western Shoshone Nation in 1863. This is what they call the Ruby Valley Treaty of Peace and Friendship.[4] It's something that we, as Shoshone, are really concerned with because the federal government signed this treaty with us. Under that document they set aside 26 million acres of land for the Shoshone to roam and to hunt on, because the government has said, "this is going to be your land for you to take care of."

Like if they owned the land from the beginning. That was Shoshone land to begin with. This is something that they should understand. They're the visitors here. They made all different kinds of rules like they're giving us something that belongs to them, but they know it didn't belong to them. We Shoshone people are the caretakers of this land. We should be the ones making the law, saying what they can do, what they can't do. They're the ones that say under that law, the treaty law as they call it, that they should be taking care of our land. Not to be giving it away or selling it. They haven't shown us that they own the land. They never have and they never will.

One time the Shoshone roamed this country before the Europeans came into this country and divided us. According to the Shoshone people we roamed in seven different states, California, Nevada, Utah, Idaho, Montana, Wyoming, and Colorado. This was Shoshone territory, where they roamed and hunted for different things like buffalo in the east, salmon in the north, and they even went down to the coast of California near where San Diego is today. The 1863 treaty restricted the land on which the Shoshone roamed and told us we were a different tribe from each other, Western, Eastern, Northern, and Southern, but we were all one Shoshone tribe at that time. They wanted to divide and conquer us, they're still trying to divide us today.

When the treaty was signed, they said this was the law of the land. Maybe they forgot what they said, or maybe they forgot what they wrote down in the treaty agreement. This is something we, the Shoshone people, are going by because they agreed to it, that they were going to take care of our land. They said, "we're going to take care of your people, we're going to put a reservation aside for you so we can teach you how to make your own living." They put reservations up and told us, "this is your reservation, you can do whatever you want on this reservation." But today we're paying just like anybody else. We have to pay our way on the reservation, and yet the government says, "you are immune to taxes and you've got hunting rights and fishing rights."

It's not so. I have never seen those things happening.[5]

They're trying their best to misuse the law that they have put here on the land. They don't allow us to go on the land and gather our pine nuts. Their law reads that we can only harvest twenty-five pounds of pine nuts.[6]

Who are they to tell us that? When we have lived on this land and survived on pine nuts for thousands if not millions of years. They say they're going to put in more money for Indian improvement throughout the country. How many people, how many reservations got improvement from the money that Congress allocated? What about the rest of the people living off the reservations or outskirts of town? When you're not recognized by the Bureau of Indian Affairs today, you're nobody. You can't enter an Indian hospital, because you're not an enrolled member of the federally recognized tribe. Our rights have been taken away from us. Like our sweat lodges. They told us we were doing evil things. This is a very important thing that we do to cleanse our body, open up our pores in our body, and praying to each other. Same with the Sun Dance. They outlawed the Sun Dance in Fort Hall, Idaho, in 1911, telling us we were doing evil things. But the Indian people continued to do their Sun Dance even though they were being attacked by the Indian police and the Sun Dance leaders put into jail. They didn't officially allow the Sun Dance again until 1926.[7]

This is something that has to be brought back and which is coming back stronger than before, but we, the people, cannot be misusing those things. If we do, we are going to lose the whole way in which it was put here for the gifted people to heal the sickly.

Fasting on a hill or on top of a mountain is also very important and something our forefathers talked about and did, but today we don't really understand the meaning of it.

Those are the reasons why throughout the world somebody else is making money from those things. It's not put on this Earth to make money from. It's put on this Mother Earth to heal the sick people.

That's what it was for, not to be shown or used as a plaything. It's a very important religious way of life.

It's very important for the older people to get together and talk about the past. This is what we have learned from the older people before us, to talk about what we came through. As a people we were never allowed to be together to talk about different things. The federal government always said to us that we, the Native people, should never be together to talk about things, because they wanted to control us. But today we're getting together and talking about those things.

We're the ones today, when we speak out, we're put behind bars. Look what they have done so far to the Native people. Stopped all our leaders speaking out, they put them behind bars and forgot about them. Although they know they didn't do anything, but they say that they are to blame for certain things. They don't want to hear the truth. My way of looking at it, the leaders throughout the country, they're not thinking about the people. They should be beautifying it better than what we're doing so far. They should be really taking care of it.

Why did they take us prisoners and march us from one end of the country to the other? Holding us as prisoners, telling us we cannot talk our Native tongue, we cannot play our Native games. We, the Native people, the caretakers, have got a right here on this land, but we're the ones that are suffering. Maybe this is the reason why they keep telling us Native people, "we're going to put nuclear waste on your land." Is that protecting the land like they said they were going to do under that treaty? I really don't think so. I think they're trying to destroy our spiritual grounds, our burial sites.

Digging Up Remains

The Native remains that have been found have been put there by us because we have to put them away in the Mother Earth. This is where we come from, and this is where we're going to have to go back to. Those are the reasons why our people have put the remains of a human wherever their life ends. So somewhere down the line we're doing wrong by digging them up. Throughout the country, the remains have been found, brought to the surface, and they don't know what to do with them, so they show it to the public. People have never done those things before, and now we're doing those things. We know they're the remains of a human. Why do we have to bring those up and study them? That's part of our remains, we come from those remains. Their resting place should never be disturbed.

Today I see that most of the museums around the world, in their basements, they've got human remains. In some places they're in jars, somewhere else they're in boxes, somewhere else they're in glass so the people can look at them. Is it good to look at Indian bones? Are we making money at that?

The artifacts are the same way. The artifacts that they're finding throughout the country, whether it's beads, arrowheads, part of a bone, whatever it is. People are finding those things and digging them up and bringing them to the attention of the public by saying, "this is Indian jewelry, Indian beads, Indian arrowheads." Remember those arrowheads kept us alive at one time, 'cause that's what's what we had to use to kill our game. Arrowheads were something that we had to use to survive on. It gave us food. It was used once before, but it should never be used again. We Native people appreciate the arrowheads wherever we find them. We don't try to pick them up or make jewelry out of them. Today, we see people wearing arrowheads around their ears and around their neck. Those are the reasons why my forefathers sang about the arrowheads and how important they were, to make sure they're happy just like anything else, because they've got a spirit from the beginning. They were sung to, they were talked to, they made sure they took a life of an animal or whatever because they were told to do those things. When they did see them lying on the ground, they left them alone. They didn't pick them up.

4 | Travels Across Newe Land

At Currant Creek Mountain in Nevada, our forefathers, our ancestors, have written something on the rocks to give us advice.

It's really hard to understand what this is about, but it is something that the people must have known and understood. The rimrocks up there have got a song, but it's a totally different kind of song than I have ever heard before. Willy Blackeye was an Indian doctor from Duckwater, and when he and I went up here, he told me the same thing, that there's a song up there. He didn't understand it either, but he said it's a song that's really beautiful. He sung it once before, and I know it's a song that's about the aliens that come here. I'm pretty sure that's what it is. Whenever I've come up here the rock is always clean, it is always swept, the little rocks are always away from the drawings as if someone or something is preserving the drawings. But today we, the people, don't understand what the writings say or what it means or what it's telling us to do. I hope someday we will understand what they were saying and what they were giving us. I don't know how to read those things, because it was put there by our ancestors a few thousand years ago.

Sometimes when you see an animal figure or a water figure, lightning, rain, plant life, they're showing us their writing on the rocks.

Another place where the Native people have written on the rocks is in Hiko Canyon, near Ely. Over there a large footprint was put on the wall by the power of Nature or maybe the power of a human. My people used to tell me that a long time ago the humans used to be much bigger than they are now. They would stand about nine feet tall. Maybe this is how the large foot got to be on the rock, because the people at that time would work with the Nature and understand how to work with the rocks.

These writings explain something to us, but today we got so modern we don't even know how to explain what it means. We know a few like the outline of mountain sheep, mountain lions, the snake, the river, the power of lightning, the trees, and the canyons.

Some of the pictures have been painted over by the non-Indians. They have tried to change the way it was put there. They put their initials on it. The writings are still there, but we're losing all of those things because somebody is always carving what they think on top of what the Native people have put there. So you see how important it is to keep this alive, to try to teach each other what it is and the directions or messages that were put there by our forefathers.

Lehman Caves

The Native people have used this cave for a thousand years or maybe more. This is what they call Wheeler Mountain, near Ely in Nevada. Inside of this mountain, in the caves, is where the Native people congregated and had their burial sites. This is where they discussed secret things. It's dark in the caves, but there is a light if you know how to use those things. My people always say, "when you pray to the Nature, to the Mother, it can give you a light."

It can give you water in there, pure water, and it can make your voice not heard by anybody. The caves are a very important part of our life, because this is where we connect with our Mother. The Mother gives us direction, energy, and gives us what we need.

Those are the reasons why it's been a hidden cave for many, many years. Nobody knew about them apart from the Native people. The tunnels go in there for miles. They don't end. But now the National Park Service owns them, and they're charging money for entrance into the caves. The Native people didn't charge anything for them.

They learned from the caves. It gave them advice. But today we're using it the wrong way. We're using it to make money. It wasn't put there for us to make money from.

Living in Death Valley

The Shoshone people at one time established themselves in Amargosa Valley, near where the town of Amargosa in southeastern California is today. There was a spring there at that time, and the Native people wandered from one spring to the other. They had their camp there during the winter months. It was important for them to come to this part of the country during the winter months because it was warmer. During the summer months they would migrate toward the north, where it's cooler. They had to follow their food, in other words.

They were forced to move from Amargosa Valley when the Tonopah to Tidewater railroad started in 1907. When the railroad came in, the non-Indian people moved in. When the mines started in that area, Amargosa began to grow. There were a lot of people working on the railroads and taking care of the engines. The Indians needed water, and this was the only water from Amargosa to the town of Shoshone, forty or so miles away, so this is why they camped there. When the train started to come through that part of the country, the Indians moved themselves from there to what they call Furnace Creek. They camped at Furnace Creek for I don't know how many years, and they made sure they camped where the water was, at the beginning of the spring in Furnace Creek, in the mouth of Death Valley, going from Amargosa into Death Valley. There was plenty of water going down in there. They had plenty to eat, because there was all different kinds of food and animals there.

But at Furnace Creek they were moved again, because miners came in wanting water and they took over where they were camped. The Native people didn't want to associate with them because they were scared of them. At that time we were being scalped by the miners and the trappers for bounty money. So they continued to move on down below Furnace Creek. They camped there on the creek bed where the creek was running from Furnace Creek. They lived there for many years, and then they moved again from there, I would say about one quarter of a mile from where they were camped into what they call now the Furnace Creek Ranch. In 1936 the Bureau of Indian Affairs (BIA) and the National Park Service moved them again from there to where they're located now, south of Furnace Creek Ranch, and the BIA built homes for them out of mud cinder blocks. That's an adobe house, in other words.

Not too long ago, I would say in the early 1980s, the government demolished some off those adobe homes and set up trailer homes for them on wheels, thinking they were going to move them again someday, to where, nobody knows.

So this is what my people went through for many, many years, moved from one place to the other because somebody wanted the land that they were surviving on.

It was very, very wrong of the United States government to do these things to the Native people. They didn't appreciate them. They wanted to take over the land and move them from one place to the other. I think this is wrong.

But recently, some of the Timbisha Shoshone people in Death Valley have asked for more land, so in November 2000 Congress passed a law granting seven thousand acres of land to the tribe, which they now manage with the National Park Service.[1]

This is very important for the Indian people living there in Death Valley. I hope that they continuously live on that land, enjoy the land, and continuously raise a family there, because we need to be recognized by the federal government.

Shoshone Caves

There are caves right out of the town of Shoshone in Southern California, at the entrance to Death Valley, where the Shoshone people used to spend their winter. They are round holes, going into the hillside, where the Native people would live in December, January, February, and then in March they would move north to someplace cooler. That is, until the miners came along and saw those caves dug in the hillside and decided to make a home for themselves. When the Indians came back the following winter, they were already occupied by somebody else, so they continued to move on. The Native people made the caves a nice, square hole. They even put a door on them by covering them with cloth.

They relied on these caves for survival. It was the perfect kind of place to live in winter when the temperatures didn't drop below freezing. At that time there were a lot of animals here like elk, rabbits, sagehen, squirrels, antelope, and deer. But when the mines used different kinds of chemicals, then they killed some of these animals. Radiation from the Nevada Test Site also dried up the land, so that the water disappeared and the animal life that relied on that water disappeared also.

Stoneburger Creek

Stoneburger Creek, in Monitor Valley, Nevada, is where the Indians used to camp long ago. It's still owned by the Shoshone people.

This was an important place because there was a lot of food here at one time. They had a lot of spring water, they had chokecherries, they had currant berries, they had buckberries, they had plenty of deer.

This is why the Shoshone people are really trying to protect that land from the miners, from the ranchers or somebody piping that water away from them.

In the 1930s the people were pushed away from here by the Bureau of Indian Affairs, who told them they could take care of them better if they were in one place. So some people were moved to the Yomba Reservation, some were moved to Battle Mountain colony and Ely colony.

It's very important for the Indian people to still go up there on this land where our ancestors used to be at one time. We used to have our pine-nuts ceremony there at one time, but now it doesn't have pine nuts, it doesn't have chokecherries, it doesn't have currant berries, buck berries, or rose berries. Those things are gone, they're dying because of the chemicals on the land.

Moores Station

My ancestors, at one time, lived in what we call Moores Station in Hot Creek Valley, between Currant Creek and Tonopah, Nevada. An underground nuclear test has been done about two and a half miles from here in 1968.[2]

There's writing on the rocks there that the Native people have put there to show that they were here at one time. The nuclear testing has created problems for the growth of all the living things here, like the pine nuts that we survived on, as well as contaminating the water.

South from here, when they set that bomb off in an underground test, it lifted the ground a mile in diameter with about seven to ten feet settlement of the Earth.

I hope you people can realize that the Native people lived here, but they were chased out of their home territory. They relied on this little tiny canyon, but when the testing was done here, my people got moved out and everything else moved out. All the living things disappeared, and today I hope the Nature itself can bring them back somehow.

North from here, there's a little tiny lake called Moores Station Lake. The fish are going crazy there, they're jumping up and down all the time. They don't have any backbones, their meat is spoiled, in other words, as a result of the nuclear testing.

Lunar Crater

I think it's very important that people know that a meteorite came into this part of the country, near Warm Springs, Nevada, a long time ago. The Shoshone people used to travel through this part of the country.

This is something that my people have talked about for many, many years, and they said that at one time, that place was very hot. You couldn't go down into that crater then because it was so hot.

They'd say it was just like being in an oven. It's about four thousand feet across and about four hundred feet deep. They said, when it was cold during the winter months, that even when it snowed, no snow stayed there, only steam came out of that crater. There was also a kind of blue light there in the crater.

Long ago there were plenty of springs in that part of the country, but when the meteorite came down several years after that, the cold-water springs dried up. When the meteorite came into that part of the country, it had a reason to come down, so it put something on the Earth.

Spiritual Grounds

Rock Creek, near Battle Mountain, Nevada, is something that was put there by the Nature. We call it *bah-tza-gohm-bah,* or otter water, because there used to be a lot of otters that lived in the water at one time.

It's a healing place for us. This is where we have our gatherings. Praying to the Nature, praying to the water, praying to the canyon, and praying to the humans in the rock watching the place all the time. On the top of the Eagle Head rock is where we put the people who are fasting. If somebody is sickly or somebody is gifted, losing their way or getting away from their gift, then this is the time we put them up there on top of the Eagle Head so they can get back their strength again that was given to them by the Nature. Those are the reasons why we have our gathering there, to keep that canyon alive and to keep it strong and healthy. The water there is very important, the canyon is very important. Singing to that canyon, talking to that canyon, praying to that canyon is a very important part of our life because it's put there by the Nature to heal our sickness. The people that are sick can heal themselves if they ask the canyon to do the wonderful things it has done for us for thousands and thousands of years. This is where some of the Native people from that area, when they passed on to a different world, this is where they put them to rest. Quite a few people have been put to rest in that particular canyon. It's important for us to keep that canyon alive because it's our spiritual grounds and our burial site, where we can pick up songs and pick up advice.

The spiritual grounds throughout the country are really important for us. We have to keep them alive, keep singing songs to them, because they're the ones that have kept us alive for thousands of years. And they're going to have to be used again by us, because we cannot afford to go with the modern way of life today. Modern sickness is something that we can't do anything with, because we're poor people, we don't have any insurance. So we have to rely on the Nature. The Nature is the one that's kept us alive for millions of years before.

Another important place for the Shoshone people at one time and today is Castle Rock in Boise, Idaho. This is where the Indian people used to camp a long time ago. There's a rock in the shape of an Indian man's head with an eagle sitting on top of it. There's a burial site along the foothills. There's quite a few of them, in fact, and this is why many people have supported us in saving this Eagle Rock from property developers. It's a very special place for the Native people. The Boise Shoshone have lived here for many, many years. It used to have hot water here, a hot spring, but the public has been digging it up and now they're warming their houses in downtown Boise with that hot water. We would like to have this place preserved because our forefathers have taught us to keep it clean and healthy, and this is what we have to start teaching our young. Our young are the ones that's going to have to be living here and to understand our way of life that we had here once before. This is something that I have learned from my people and tried to preserve, the way it was from the beginning.

Mineral Water at Monroe

In Monroe, Utah, my people gathered at one time to enjoy and pray for the hot water that was put here by the Nature, because this is a healing water. The Native people came from all parts of the country to do their ceremonies here. It was important for us to meet here, especially when we had a sickness of some kind, because that water comes from within the Nature to the top of this Earth.

The dome was put here by the Nature. At one time it probably had a cave underneath it. As the years went by, it covered the entrance underneath this big dome. That dome must be at least fifty feet high by one hundred or so feet in diameter. The water pours over this to make the crystals around it to shut the entrance underneath it.

I was invited to go over there and look at this, because some of my people have been massacred there at one time by the cavalry, by the United States Army, in other words. Some were taken prisoner, some were massacred, for what reason? Because they wanted to control that water. They should have come to join us and enjoyed the hot water with us instead of taking our life.

Somewhere the United States government should say, "we're sorry we have done this to you for no reason." People were just living there, enjoying the mineral water, and then the cavalry came along and killed them or took them as prisoner. Then the United States government came along and tried to destroy the mineral water that was coming out of the ground by using dynamite and blowing it up. But the water is continuing to come out of the ground today.

Snake River

My people used to survive on the salmon at Thousand Falls, Idaho, because they were easier to catch due to the fresh water falling into the Snake River. But today things have changed, as all the springs are disappearing into manmade pipes that have changed the way in which the Nature has put it here. Today we, the people, have to realize how important the food was at that time, because the fish were put here by the Nature for us to survive on. They have to survive on the springs coming from the mountainside. The mountain springs give them food because the Nature has put it there for them to survive on, and this is why the salmon are here. My people came here to get their salmon supply for the winter months. They dried them and took them home to wherever they came from, because we didn't survive on one thing, we survived on a lot of different kinds of plants and animals.

We, the people, have to support the way the Nature put things here. If we don't take care of it, we're not going to be able to survive —we've already seen that happening. Like the salmon, now is not here. There might be a few in Snake River, but most of them have left this part of the river, because the water has been piped.

Further downstream is where Snake River flows over a lava rock, where the lava flow, at one time, went down into the river. This is where the Indian people camped during the winter, because the lava rocks kept the valley warm. The Native people loved to be here during the winter, but now, today, it's totally different because people have built houses, changing the looks of the canyon. Today we are suffering because the fish are dying in the river. The river is not clean anymore because we're dumping everything into that river. The sewage is going into the river itself because there are so many houses in this canyon. When you see it, then you realize how important it is, because there's a lot of springs here in this canyon, a lot of clean water coming out. Let's not destroy it anymore.

Twin Rivers

At what they call Twin Rivers in Smokey Valley, Nevada, there's a north river where at one time the Native people lived, farmed and made their living for thousands of years. They kept things clean. At one time the north canyon and the south canyon both had fish in the river. At one time the Indian people survived off this land. There was a lot of animal life in this canyon. They had a lot of food to eat, but today when I see this river, it doesn't have any life. I can't see any fish or anything. It's been overused by people. They have eliminated all different kinds of life. I don't see any berries of any kind. There used to be berries here at one time, but today we don't have any because they've been overused by people. This is what we, as a Native people, have always said: "If you overdo something without appreciating it, it can disappear."

So this is what's happening. You see it, we all see it. The animal life has been chased away from its habitat because we overused them. We're not appreciating why the Indian people took care of what they had in this particular canyon. We're going to have to appreciate those things.

The pine nuts in this canyon, which my people survived on, are not here anymore—there's no cones. They haven't been here for the last few years. There's been no cones from last year and the year before, so we know something's wrong because there's no more food for anything to survive on. This is what we're saying as Native people. We have to bring those things back with our prayer. Our prayer is the only thing that we've got left today.

PART III

Newe Wisdom

5 | Healing with Our Prayers

've worked with many, many Indian doctors throughout the country. Many of them are from different states, different tribes. All the healers that I know of, they all work with the spirit of an animal, a bird, rocks, whatever. The Spirit is the one that tells us what to do, what to give, the kinds of herbs to use, or what to tell the person we're praying for so that they may have direction or advice. Like myself, I have asked many, many people either to get a magpie tail or a pure white pebble of rock. It doesn't have to be crystal, but it does have to come from the riverbed. This is the message that the Spirit may tell me to pass onto whoever's sick. I tell them to maybe take a bath or find something that the Spirit has told me that they must look for. Our healers were given their power from Nature or either that it's in their bloodline. If your parents are healers, then that blood can continue, but we have to take care of ourselves. We cannot misuse those things. We have to make sure that we keep ourselves clean as much as we can.

We understand what's going on, but it's not for us as an individual to tell people. It's up to the Spirit to tell the message that they want to put out to people. This is how we work. We work with Nature. The songs, the words, everything comes from the Nature or the Spirit. This is why my songs are different from other people's songs. So we make sure we don't misuse the sickly person and make sure they don't misuse us. When we give advice to the sick person, what the Spirit has told us to pass on to them, then they have to follow it. If they don't follow that advice, then what good are we? This is when the spirit of an animal turns against us. I've been through it many, many times, trying to tell the people what to get, what to do. If they don't do what I advise them to do, it comes back onto a person. The person gets hit by something that's very dangerous. I can lose my power overnight if somebody doesn't follow the way the Spirit has said for me to pass on.

So those are the things that we had to follow. It's really important that we, as spiritual people, don't go out there and say, "I do this and I do that." You don't see any spiritual people bragging, "I can do this and I can do that." Let's not say I'm a healer, I'm a pipe carrier, I'm a pouch carrier. Maybe you're just make-believing in what you're doing. You're not actually working with the Nature. Let's not play that game. That's a dangerous game to play, when you say you're this and you're that.

The reason is, we don't know until we work on somebody. Then the Spirit tells us what to do. It's not me that doctors people, it's the Spirit. All I can do is have a knowledge of people, what kind of sickness they have. The Spirit is the one that put all of those things here on the Earth.

For us Native people, the Nature has put all different kinds of herbs here for us to use. Those are the reasons why we follow the Nature Way of Life. At certain times the Nature doesn't tell us anything either, because that's their way. This is why I'm telling you, don't think I'm the one that makes the rules and regulations. I don't. Some of you have been to my ceremonies and have prayed for all the living things. I have to pray for those things. Those things were put here for us to use. Those are the reasons why I sing about those things, to make them happy. Let me tell you a little bit about my way of singing songs in the morning.

Darkness/Doogupi

The very first thing I sing about is the darkness and how important that darkness is. My forefathers survived under darkness, your forefathers survived under darkness. If it wasn't for darkness, your enemies would have wiped your forefathers out. We wouldn't be here today if it wasn't for darkness. So that makes me feel good to sing about the darkness, to make that darkness happy, because it was put here for a reason. The darkness is still used by a lot of creatures on this Earth of ours. This is why the Nature has put darkness on this Earth. Some creatures only move during darkness, some creatures only move during moonlight. Some creatures only move during daylight. It's really important to think about how important the darkness is, for the creatures that run away from us. We're the enemies today for all the animal life. Under daylight we have taken many, many creatures' lives, and today they're trying to move under darkness away from us.

Water/Bah

I sing about water, how important water is. If it wasn't for water, everything would have dried up. Today we've begun to see that happening throughout the country because the spirit of water is dying throughout the world. We, the people, are going to have to ask the spirit of the water to continue to keep itself clean and strong so that it keeps us healthy and clean. Everything uses water. I don't care what it is. Everything comes from water. If it wasn't for water, there'd be no firewood, there'd be no rocks, there'd be no Earth. The Earth might be here, but there'd be no life on it. So we all rely on water. Those are the reasons why I sing about water and how important it is to flow over the Earth and to give life to all the living things. We have to appreciate that water. If it wasn't for water, how long could we live?

We might say we can get all kinds of soda pop and drinks from the store, but remember they are all made from water. Animal life has to have water, bird life has to have water, plant life has to have water, everything's connected to water.

I sing about those things to make the water spirit happy, so it will continue to flow. Since we don't appreciate the water, now it has begun to get away from us.

Plant Life/Dewesungup

I sing about the plant life throughout the world. We use all different kinds of plant life for different things, some for shade, some for birds to nest in, some plant life produces berries and fruit. Each year they get older, each year they produce something for us. They enjoy doing that for us, but we're the ones that should enjoy them by talking to them, singing to them, and asking their life to continue. We're the ones supposed to have the voice to ask their spirit to continue their life. This is why our forefathers were really strong people who lived a healthier life, because they took care of what they had and took care of the plant life.

Rocks/Bunn Narumbichee

I sing about rocks, how important rocks are. Just think, how many creatures live in the rocks? Those rocks take care of those creatures and let them live within the rock. Different kinds of creatures live in the rocks. They enjoy the rocks and the rocks enjoy them because the Nature has put it there for them.

In my prayer, I'm saying in my Native tongue, every time the rock rolls, it chips some, it leaves some. From a big boulder, it becomes gravel, from gravel to sand, from sand to dirt. That's how important rocks are.

My people have used rocks for healing. All human beings at one time used rocks for healing purposes, by heating up rocks and putting it wherever your pain is. That rock will take away your pain from you if you ask.

So I sing to the rocks, to make the rock spirit happy so the rock can continue to support us and we can enjoy the life of rocks. You can hear songs and voices from rocks. It's very important when that rock sings songs that we listen to it talk. Sometimes when a baby was sick, they'd lean the baby up against rocks and ask that rock to take the sickness away. The baby might cry a little, but after awhile that rock starts to work on it and when it wakes up the sickness is gone.

Rocks are very important because they were medicine at one time. They cater to all different kinds of sickness, and they deliver life on this Earth. As Indian people, we had to heat up rocks and put them in the ground and lay a woman that's going to have a baby on those rocks with all different kinds of herbs on it. The midwife, as we call her today, delivers life onto the Earth, and she talks and sings to the baby as it's being born. Your name is given the day, the minute that you are born. You're either connected to a tree, an animal, a flower, a butterfly, bird, water, and so forth. They see that you are connected to those things the minute you are born. Until the Europeans came and changed our name, then they called us Joe, Henry, Frank, you name it. That's not our name. Just like my name is not Corbin Harney, because that was given to me by the European people. My name is totally different. My name is Dabashee, which means the "flare of the sun at sunrise and sunset."

Wind/Neyipe

Then I sing about the wind, how important wind is. It gives us life. We breathe that wind, that air. Air is very important. Without air we wouldn't have anything to breathe, we wouldn't live very long. This is why we, the people, have to ask the wind to not harm us but to continuously give us fresh air.

Wind blows in a circle. It blows in three layers, one above the Earth and so forth down the line.

If we don't appreciate the air, where are we going to get air? No human can ever make air that you can survive on. A machine might develop air. But you cannot survive on that air for long because it's not purified, it's not clean. The air is what the Nature has put here. A little breeze, if we ask that breeze to give us a fresh air, give us a clean mind, it can do those things because if we ask, it can do a beautiful thing.

Then I sing about horned toads.[1] To us Native people the horned toad is a very important creature. At one time we used to bleed each other, and this is where the horned toad comes in. If you tell the horned toad you want a sick person's blood to be drained, he can drain it for you because he's got a sharp knife on his side. When you put your foot on him, he can cut your foot open on the bottom and drain your blood for you. When you've got too much blood, like high blood pressure or if you've got sick blood, then this horned toad will bleed you, he'll take the sickness out of you.

These are the very important things that this little creature can do because he was put here to do this work. He wasn't just a horned toad that runs around out there, he had a lot of work put here for him to do. We Native people enjoyed working with this little creature at one time, we appreciate him.

When he gets through bleeding you and he takes all of the bad blood out of your system, then he'll turn black and purple in color and he gets bigger. When you take your foot away from him, then you have to give him something.

So I know, I have seen it done, I have seen it work on a lot of people. For instance if your leg is swollen up from bad blood, he can drain it for you if you ask him, but you're the one that's going to have to tell him why you want him to work on you. A horned toad even told me I should be singing about him. I have talked to the horned toad, and the horned toad said, "well I'm ready anytime when you ask me to help you."

So all the little creatures and whatever kind of medicine is out there, we have to talk to it and tell it the reason why we're taking their life. Same with the little horned toad. If you ask him to drain your blood, he can. He can doctor you because he is a doctor. He's a doctor to the other animals, he's a doctor to the human race, and he's someone we will have to rely on in the future.

Sun/Dabeh

Then I sing about the sun, how important that sun is. I appreciate the sun. We get heat from it, we get light from it, it gives us energy. It gives life to all the living things on this planet of ours. If it wasn't for sun, this Mother Earth would have been just a ball of ice, everything would be frozen on it. Ice would be on it a few hundred miles deep. This is why I have to sing about it, to make sure it's happy.

Bear/Wurra

One time I met a bear out of Fort Bragg, California, up in the mountains, walking down the trail. He was coming up that trail and I was going down that trail. We came face to face. I didn't know what to do, whether to run or stay, but I remembered that I was told never to run away from a bear because he can outrun you. But if you sing to him and talk to him, then he'll sit down and he'll listen to you. This is what I've been told about a bear from the beginning of my life. So when I did talk to him and sing to him, he sat down and I sat down. He was there a few minutes I would say, and when I did sing songs to him then he finally, within maybe five, maybe seven minutes, got up, and I didn't know what to do, but I kept on talking and telling him that he's part of me, I'm part of him, we're here together, so you have to listen to me and I'll listen to you. The bear got up and turned around and went back down the trail the way he'd come up. I stood there for a long time, thinking should I follow him or not? I finally decided I'd better go see where he disappeared to. The trail went around a big, huge rock, and he went around it and I saw him disappear. I thought I'd better go around there and go see. I followed his tracks to where that trail went around this huge rock. From there I decided I'd better leave instead of trying to follow him, so I turned around and went back up the trail.

I was told about the bear from the beginning of my life, because I remember my people talked about how bears have taken care of humans at one time, a long time ago. They took care of a human if they were left behind when the people were roaming from one place to the other. Maybe sometimes the mommy would run out of milk or the mommy passed on, so nobody took care of the little one. When the bear heard the little baby crying, then he went over there and picked up the little one and took it to his den. Not only the bear took care of people, everything did at one time. They watched over them, they gave them what they had to raise them. This is how the animal life treated the people at one time. Since we haven't been doing anything for them, or praying for their food, now they're coming down to where we're at, looking for something to eat.

It's really sad to see the bear or any animal hungry out there. This is why I sing songs about the bear. The bear spirit tells me, "I'm out there crying because I don't have much food. I'm searching for food." The bear song is about the bear roaming this Mother Earth, but he's crying because he's running out of water, he's running out of food. So he's asking us, "give me a lending hand, pray for my food." That's what he's saying.

Medicine Rock

I'm going to talk a little bit about Medicine Rock, over there in Nevada City in California, where the people used to go to heal the sickness from their body by asking the rock to heal them from their sickness. This was a very important rock for the Native people in that part of the country, because this is how they healed their sickness before the Europeans ever came into this part of the continent. The European people came into that part of the country, the miners and the trappers, and they heard the Native people used this rock for healing their sickness. But the European people decided to build a home on this rock, right next to it. Now that rock is covered by a house that was built on top of it. So the Native people were chased away from their healing rock.

The people that built the house thought it was going to help them, but instead of that it kept them awake at nights, they couldn't sleep because something bothered them, they didn't know what. The chairs and the tables moved around in the house. They thought they moved around in the house, but in the morning they saw that things were in the same position.

This rock had a healing power for the Indian people. They had to talk to it and it had to give them a special message before they could receive a healing. It doesn't just happen by looking at it, it had to have a special way of doing those things. It's not there just for a plaything, it's a healing stone, a healing rock. It can heal you because the Nature put it there. It's got the power to heal you from your sickness. Those are the reasons why people long ago used something the Nature has put there to heal their sickness.

We didn't have hospitals, we didn't have modern doctors as they're called today. We had to rely on the Nature, the healing rocks, healing water, healing trees, healing animals. It's not only here in Nevada City, these healing rocks are all over the country.

Doctor Water/Poo-Ha-Bah

Hot mineral water was really important for my people at one time. We call it Doctor Water, or Poo-Ha-Bah in my language. They looked for mineral water throughout the country. They traveled long distances to get into hot mineral water. The mineral water is something that we have to work with. It's good for different kinds of sickness, rheumatism, arthritis, broken bones, and aches of all different kinds. The animals, they get into hot water and stand there for hours if they've got hoof disease of some kind. This is how wild animals cure themselves from those kinds of sickness.

Now everybody has begun to search for hot mineral water. But at one time this hot water and all the living things the Nature provided for us never said to us, "pay me first before you use me." This is one thing that I've been taught by my older people, that I cannot be charging people for healing because the Nature didn't tell us to. The Nature has put those things here for us, for us to take care of. We cannot let this die out. If we do, look at the food that comes from this water, look at the medicine that comes from this water. All the living things need our support, so we're the ones that are going to have to do the best we can to understand why we have to work together.

6 | Surviving on Nature's Medicine

Indian Balsam/Toza

Toza is one of our medicines. It's a big, green root about four feet tall contained within a big clump of roots. It grows under the ground. Our name for it is *toza*. I don't know the English name for it.[1]

At a certain time of the year it has to be harvested. Not anytime, because it relies on the Nature, it relies on the seasons. When the flower is blooming on the plant, then this is the time that they have a lot of sap in the root. We, as Native people, boil it in water and drink it for colds, sore throats, or soreness on your body. I have used it many, many times for soreness or on a big cut. You can put the roots of that *toza* on those things, it can heal your body and heal your skin on account of the sap in it. We have used this *toza* for bites of mosquitoes, ants, spiders, and for rattlesnake bites. It can draw out the poison in your stomach or in your system because it's good for your blood. Those are the reasons why the animal life, when it first starts out in spring, likes to eat it and so do we! We use it for salad. It really tastes good in spring, just like any other food that we used to survive on. This is something that my people used for feeding a little baby by putting a little bit of this in their food or in their milk. A lot of people have used it in water to clear the water, and when you see that sap floating, the grease part of it on the water, this is the time they used it for rheumatism, arthritis, or bone aches. They put it in the water and boiled it for fifteen to twenty minutes.

Today I see a lot of people still using it to smudge themselves with. I know from way back, my people used this *toza* to smudge themselves with. It's even documented in writing that the army, in the 1700s, was given orders to issue out blankets that were contaminated with smallpox to the Native people because they wanted to get rid of them.[2]

Even when I was a little boy in the 1920s, I remember seeing my people using the smoke of this *toza* to smudge some blankets that they had been given and then use them. This killed the diseases that were in those blankets.

So *toza* is something that has been used by us for many, many years. I hope that we can continue to pray for them and talk to them, ask them to continue to grow and be strong, so that way they can still help us and we can help them.

Biscuit Root/Zoyiga

What the white man calls a big root, in our Shoshone language we call *zoyiga*. A lot of people have the same name who come from an area where there's lots of *zoyiga*. Zoyiga is a tribe that's in northern California, going into southern Oregon and southern Idaho.

It's a very important food. We Native people used to get together and go to certain areas where it was growing and see how much we could gather. They're big roots. You can only harvest them in June. In the middle of July you'll never find them again, because the Nature has put it there for us to harvest, to dig them out, in June. This is something that we made flour out of. We made the flour into something similar to the modern-day food, rice cakes. They made those things just like that but a little heavier than a rice cake. It's light in weight, but when you make flour out of them you put a little water in them, then you can make a bread out of that. Some creatures dig them out and eat them when they're still raw, but we dig them out of the ground and put them into a few sacks. Some people might get twenty sacks, thirty sacks and then dry them. Then the skin part of it comes off and it's totally white. When we dry them and make a disc patty, then we can carry a whole bunch of them. They're heavy when they're still in the ground or when they're wet. We had to have a ceremony for them and ask them to continue their growth and to never let us down. They're fluffy, light in weight. You can eat one disc, and that gives you energy. This is something that we don't harvest anymore, because it only appears in June, only in certain areas, and like everything else it's disappearing.

Wild Roses/*Tsiavi*

We Native people have used wild roses for many different things. The berries we used to eat by taking the seeds out and drying them. The seed is something that we can't eat, because it makes you itch when you eat them.

Wild roses are also what identifies us as Shoshone.

Maybe some of you people have seen the roots of wild roses. They look like a red ball, sometimes they're pink. We used it to make a red dye, but most of the time we used the roots to clarify our blood, to heal our blood veins. If you cut that red ball open, a liquid that looks like blood runs out of it. We used to put it in a little bit of water and let that red liquid drain out. Some people cut it into slices and dry it, just like beets. It is very important for our blood, our health, and our hearts. But again, it's got to be harvested at certain times. You don't just go out there and dig them up at any time. When they're nice and ripe, when they're nice in strength, they give you energy.

This is something that people don't understand, but you have to use it the way it was put here, you just can't do it any old way thinking it's going to help you. It's not going to do a bit of good. You have to work with the Nature and say a few words to it. You don't see many wild roses anymore because they're drying up. I hope that they can come back again so we can continue to use them, but like I say, it's up to us to make sure they continue to grow.

Peppermint/*Bahguwanah*

Wild Peppermint is something we Native people have used to rub on ourselves when we itch, and it will take away that itch. We make a tea from it to clear our stomach, to make our stomach feel better, or either we just smell it, rub it, or put it on our nose to take away a headache. This is something we can gather anywhere there's water. Along creek beds a lot of peppermint grows. When we harvest it, we like the smell of it, we like the taste of it, we put it in our food, we make tea out of it.

Peppermint is good if you've got stomach problems or diarrhea, but it's got to be wild, it can't be grown by humans, because the Nature put it there for us to use in this way.

And again, peppermint was put here for us to use not every day, but maybe thirty days out of a year, when the flowers are on them, that's when they should be harvested. When the pink flowers start out on them, sometimes they're purple, sometimes they're pink. The older it gets, the darker that pink gets. This is their time to harvest them. That's the time they've got strength to give you strength and energy. A lot of people wash their hair with it. For flakes in your hair, washing it with peppermint will settle it down for you, but it's got to be strong, it's got to be told the reason why before you take it out of the ground or harvest it. You have to tell it why you're taking its life.

Currant Berries/*Bohumpi*

I think most of us know about currant berries. Currant berries come in different colors, some are orange, some are white, some are red, some are black in color. Maybe most of you people have had currant pie or currant jam.

We had to take care of these things at one time. If we touched the berries and sampled them at any time, when they began to get ripe, with our dirt on them, then the birds would go after them and there wouldn't be any currant berries left. Those are the reasons why my people always say, "make sure you don't touch the food, our medicine, or the berries of any kind before you harvest them. If you do touch them before, then the birds will eat them all."

This is why the Native people throughout the country say you have to wait until they're ripe. Just like anything else, at certain times they're sour, certain times they're sweet.

Elderberries/Duhiembuh

Elderberries are a very important food for the birds, the animal life, and for the human beings. The Indian doctors use the wood part of the elderberry for doctoring. We suck a sickness from a person's body from the hole on the inside of this wood. Elderberries have nice, sweet berries which are blue in color, and they grow over mountains and hillsides, but they've been dying for the last few years. Now the plant has begun to dry up, and I think we all know it's dying from some kind of pollution that we're putting out there on the Mother Earth. I know the birds are sad. Their food is beginning to disappear. Elderberry has said to us, "I'm here for you, if you take care of me, I'll take care of you. If you touch me at the wrong time I might get moldy because you took me at the wrong time. If you take me, what are you going to use me for, how are you going to use me?"

These are the things that we were told. This is why we have ceremonies for them. The berries like to hear our ceremony when we're singing to them, so that they can enjoy their life just like we do. Those are the reasons why we use it for doctoring and for ceremonies. It's good for your system, it makes your stomach work better because it can digest food, when you eat a lot of it. But today it's scarce. I hope someday we realize that we might not have this elderberry, because it's already begun to dry up around the world. You people around this world are going to have to really start praying for these things in order for them to come back. We're the people with a voice. We're the people that should be thanking those things, appreciating the little berries, because everything relies on us.

Buckberries/Weeyum

There's two different kinds of buckberries, one is what we call *weeyum*.

Weeyum was a very important food for us Native people at one time. We used it for many things. We'd make gravy out of it, we'd enjoy eating it. Sometimes our healers, the doctors, would use them in their doctoring.

There used to be a lot of *weeyum* throughout the country. I remember people going all the way around Battle Mountain in Nevada, where there used to be a lot of buckberry trees. Some people would go to Yerington, Nevada. In different places they had different tastes to them. The buckberries around Battle Mountain were orange in color, the ones in Yerington were pink and reddish in color. They were sweeter than the ones around Battle Mountain. Our forefathers had to gather the buckberries at a certain time of the year and dry them for winter use. When they're dried in the winter, you can put them in hot water or you can make gravy out of them. You can make a pie out of them and you can make a cake with them, but again here, you have to talk to them.

Chokecherries/Donanbe

Chokecherries are another thing we use for our blood. They're kind of dark blue, almost black in color, and they help us to digest the food better in our digestive system. We call it our fruit. When we dry chokecherries, we can make jam out of them, we can make syrup out of them, or we can make chokecherry patties to store for use in the winter. When we make a chokecherry pudding, we have to get the seeds out by boiling it for a little while, then we squeeze the chokecherry meat from the seed itself. Then we either dry them with the seed or we grind them and make a patty. The chokecherries we use for medicine help our heart, our kidneys, our liver, and our blood. My people used chokecherries for dyeing their clothes because it's strong. Once you get it into a cloth of any kind, then it's hard to get it off. When you dry the liquid part of it, this is what we use for paint. You can also use the choke-cherry bark. Boil it until it turns red and put it on your scalp to take away dandruff.

The rabbitbrush is connected to the chokecherry. When that rabbitbrush is in full bloom, it's telling us the chokecherries are ready to be harvested, ready to be picked. This was very important.

You have to cleanse yourself and pray to the berries. "If we don't do those things," our forefathers have told us, "they can disappear," which is what we see happening today. The chokecherries are not here any more. What little chokecherry you can find here and there is scarce, because we didn't appreciate how it was put there. If you pray for it and take care of it the way the Nature put it here, it'll have more meat and little, tiny seeds. But today, since we haven't been taking care of it, it's got a big seed and not much meat, not much of anything that we can really harvest.

Acorns/Kuniape

Acorns are very important to the Native people as well as to the squirrels, the deer, and the antelopes. Acorn is something that was put here by Nature to feed all the things that survived from it. When the Native people harvested the acorns, they did their ceremonies before they went to pick the acorns off the trees. At one time the acorn didn't fall off the trees until a certain time. We used to make acorn soup, acorn bread, and acorn pudding.

There used to be a lot of acorn trees throughout the country. There used to be a lot of squirrels that put them away for the winter so that they would have food during the winter months. Same with humans. They picked acorns and then put them in the ground for winter use, just like an animal. You see squirrels running up and down a tree carrying acorns to their den or going into a hole to store acorns.

Pine nuts/Durba

The Nature put the pine tree here to bear food, what we call pine nuts, or *durba*. But these trees are dying because of all the different kinds of chemicals in the air. Pine nuts are a very important food for all the living things. Everything eats it from the ant to the birds. We, as Native people, today are looking for pine nuts throughout the country, but there's very few pine nuts left. You might see a few pine nuts here and there, but not many.

Pine nuts are a really healthy food for us, especially when they're greasy. The grease is a very important part of that pine nut. It takes care of your body, takes care of your bones, takes care of your heart. We make flour out of it, we make tacos out of it, we make bread out of it, we put it in our soup.

The pine-nut tree, when it's dead, it doesn't have much use for us. We can only use it to build a fire, because it has a good flame due to the sap in it. When the sap turns pink, we can make a gum out of it. When we chew it, that sap helps our teeth to be clean, our gums to be healthy, and stops our gums from becoming diseased.

Also, when we burn it, we use the smoke to smudge our people or we use it for different kinds of sickness. It's really important for us to think about how important pine nuts were. Some of you people enjoy eating them, some of you people enjoy cooking with them, or maybe you put them in a soup like my people have done, when they threw it in with the deer ear and boiled the deer ear or deer tail.

My people miss their pine-nuts food and so do the squirrels, the birds, the animal life because, like I say, the chemicals are killing those things, killing our food, and killing our medicine.

Harvesting Pine nuts/Durba Yickwi

The Shoshone people used to go and gather pine nuts near Austin, Nevada. Maybe a few families gathered together in a little band of maybe ten people, sometimes more. They prayed for those pine nuts before they took the cones off the tree.

April is the time that we go out and thank the tree, ask the tree to continue to grow and continue to bear those pine nuts for us. Then we get together again in June to ask the Nature to bring water to them. The Nature does those things if we ask. Then in August/ September, this is when we go out and start gathering the pine nuts, the green cones, in other words, that bear those little nuts in the cones. The people collect the pine nuts with two long poles. Those poles are about fifteen feet long. A long pole with a hook on the end of it pulls the cone off the tree. Then maybe two or three people get a whole bunch of them and get the cones on the ground. The people behind them go along and pick up the green cones. It's not easy, it's hard work.

Then someone builds a fire from the dried trees, dead trees, in other words. They make a big charcoal pit, and when it's hot enough with enough ashes, enough charcoal to make a hole in the middle of it, then this is where we dump the green pinecones into the fire. This is how they cook it overnight. But you've got to know how to cook it. If you don't know how to do it, you can burn your cones. If you know how to do it, you can cook it just enough so it'll take the sap off. Then it softens the cone and it's cooked with the steam.

Of course the charcoal is mixed with dirt, a kind of sandy dirt, and that's how it's cooked. The very next morning, before sunrise, around ten, maybe fifteen women sit around this fire and sing their songs while getting those pine nuts out of the cones. If you don't have them cooked enough then your finger's going to get sore, because the cones are hard. They don't talk much, they mostly sing their songs. Different women have different songs.

Then they put the pine nuts into a gunnysack. What they call the winnowing basket separates the bad pine nuts or the cones that don't have any pine nuts in them. They throw this basket up and down. When they're done, everybody gets their share and it gets divided among the camp. They made sure they worked together in order to have pine nuts during the winter months.

Rabbitbrush/Sewupi

Rabbitbrush is a very important brush for us Native people and the rabbits. The rabbits enjoy eating the rabbitbrush, and the bees enjoy eating the honey from the flower on the end of it. We like to take the roots of the rabbitbrush and make a gum out of it. Tastes good when you chew on it. It also cleans your teeth and it cleans your gums, it makes your gums stronger. Rabbitbrush is something we have used for different kinds of sickness.

We take the end of the flower and boil it for a very short time, maybe five to seven minutes, then we drink the liquid. This is why we like to eat rabbit. When a rabbit has eaten the rabbitbrush, then it's eaten the medicine from that plant. So when we eat the rabbit, it's got medicine inside it. If the rabbitbrush comes in full bloom, yellow, then that means the pine nuts are ready and the chokecherries are ready to harvest.

Sunflowers/Uck

Sunflower seeds are something that we have harvested during the summer months of August and September. Sunflowers have been used by my people for thousands and thousands of years. If you harvest them at the certain time of the year when they're supposed to be harvested, then they're ripe and they've got energy in them. When the flowers fall off, then the seeds start coming off easier. This is why we have to protect the sunflower, not only in one part of the country but throughout the country. We have to take care of it by talking to it and singing to it, to make sure that they continue to grow and give us strength when we eat them. We use sunflowers in several different ways. One way is to make a gravy out of them. Another way is to make flour out of them or to put them in a soup or mix them with our food.

Wild Onions/Baythus

Wild onions were put here by the Nature. The animal life and the human beings like to eat onions especially in the spring of the year. We rely on wild onions, we use them during the winter months when they are dried. But before we harvest them, before we get them out of the ground, we ask the wild onion to continue to grow so it can continue to give us onions.

One type of wild onion which is a little bit bigger in the roots and the stem is called *baythus*. Animal life, bird life, everything eats this *baythus*. Sometimes we can't eat the meat of an animal because they might have too many onions in their body. Onions are one of our medicines to begin with, so we have to take care of them.

Indian Tobacco/Newe Bahoo

We, the Indian people, have used Indian tobacco throughout the country for ceremonies. We don't smoke it every day. It's smoked at the time a healing takes place. The doctor smokes the Indian tobacco in a little pipe.

There are still a lot of tobacco plants out in the hills today, but we don't know when to gather them or how to gather them. It is something that is really important to us because it was put there by the Nature. We gather the plants, let them dry, we mash them up, then we smoke it. It's kinda sweet. It will also open up your lungs for you if you're plugged up. We pray for it and put it over the ashes of a fire, so that it would make a smoke. Because smoke has said to us at one time, "I'll carry your message for you, but you have to ask me and tell me the reason why you want to put that message out."

Long ago the white man thought the Indians were making signals with the smoke of a fire, but it wasn't them. It was the smoke itself carrying the message to another tribe so the people over the next hill or valley would know what's going on.

We have to talk to that smoke and pray to it so the smoke would bless us and carry our prayers to wherever they are needed.

Gopher/Yee-Ha-Vitch

The *yee-ha-vitch*, or gopher, is an animal that our healers have worked with for many, many years. When we pray for somebody, we usually put them on a mound of gopher dirt and ask the gopher to take the sickness away from that person. On a fresh mound that the gopher has dug up on the ground, we open up the hole and stand over it and pray for whoever is sick. Sometimes I've prayed with just the mounds of dirt because it's clean, fresh dirt coming from underneath the ground. Then that little animal likes to take those prayers and that sickness and bury it deeply within the Mother Earth. He takes that sickness away from you.

Wheat Gathering/Baye-Yickwi

Long ago, as I remember, the women used to get together during the harvesting of the wheat. Many women would take their *yandow* basket and go out there and pick the wheat that the harvesting machine didn't get. Where the machine turned in the corner, it left a lot of wheat standing, so this is where the women would harvest. At one time we had lots of wheat because the ranchers and the farmers raised a lot of wheat for their cattle and chickens.

They used to roam from one field to another following the thrashing machine wherever it went thrashing the wheat on the field. The farmers enjoyed us going behind the thrashing machine picking up the wheat, because then there would be nothing left on the field, so the birds wouldn't bother coming in to look for food. And if the farmers wanted to raise a different kind of grain in that same field, they wouldn't have to mess around with the wheat seeds left behind. This is how we made flour, by grinding the wheat by hand. We didn't have a machine that ground wheat. It had to be done with a stone.

Same with all the berries. Sometimes they had to be ground to make flour to keep us going through the winter months. Winter months were something we had to think about. This is why our forefathers had to really rustle during the summer months. In the fall of the year, when everything was there to harvest, they worked from before sunrise to dark. From dark to dark, in other words. They didn't have any spare time. They had to really hustle in order to feed their families during the winter months, because there was nowhere that we could raise our own grain. The Native people didn't have any machinery. We didn't have modern equipment at that time, but today it's totally different, it's all done by machine. At that time it was mostly done by hand, by ploughs that you held onto. Your plough had to be dragged by horses, which the Indian people didn't have many of.

Willow/*Tsur Abe*

Today throughout the world, a lot of people have seen baskets made from willow. We used those willows for a very important thing: the growth of a child. We made what we call a cradle board, or *gkoorno*. It kept the baby straight so that they wouldn't have a hunched back. The mommy used to hang the baby on a tree or lean it up against rocks in the papoose basket while she was nearby gathering food. That tree or rock would sing to the baby and talk to it and take care of it. Every hour or so the mother would go and feed the baby and check on it. Animals do the same thing with their young, there's no difference.

We made willow baskets by hand. By singing to it and talking to it, that basket became part of us. It helped us. We also used willow for headaches and dizziness. By chewing on it, you can get rid of your headache, because that's where aspirin came from to begin with. When I'm talking to a group of people, I have to have willow in my pocket or in my mouth or in my hand, because willow is something that brings peace on this Earth. It gives you peace of mind. Willow is something that everything uses. Animals like to sit around willows, they eat the bark and the leaves of the willow.

We use willows for a lot of different things. Some people used to make homes with willows. We use willow to build our sweat lodges. Even today, most of our older people go around gathering willows to make baskets.

But the willows throughout the country today have begun to die out, because we never appreciated them and we never asked their life to continue. Willows are a very important part of our life, let's take care of them.

Cottonwood Trees/*Sinabi*

The Native people really enjoyed cottonwood trees. They helped us in a lot of different ways. At one time we used cottonwood trees for our Sun Dance. Cottonwood trees are special trees. They give you sweetness when you take the bark off. There's a jelly between the bark and the tree itself that's as sweet as candy. Sometimes when you're up where there's no water, this tree will give you water. When you sit under it and take shade, in other words, from this tree, you can feel a sprinkle over you from the tree. This tree is a very important part of our life. We appreciate this tree. It gives life to all different things. The birds like to have their nest in this tree, because it gives them life so that they can survive off this tree. When you see a tree that's been damaged by somebody, they don't have any concern for life of any kind. To us Native people this tree's got a life like we do, it eats like we do, it drinks water like we do, it breathes air like we do. It sings songs to us. When you're sitting under a tree, leaning up against it, it'll give you energy, it'll give you strength. It can even heal you from your sickness if you've got a sickness, but you have to be the one to talk to the tree and tell it why you want that tree to heal you from your sickness or give you energy.

When it's dead, I don't think we would enjoy it. We have to have a tree that's alive and that gives us support, we have to take care of these trees on this Earth of ours. They were put here for us to enjoy. We have enjoyed the trees, but we shouldn't be doing what we're doing, trying to take its life, make it look bad, make the tree feel sad. This is how you kill the life of a tree by damaging it. This tree took care of us for many, many years. We're the ones that should be taking care of it, not trying to destroy it. Someday when they're not here, what are we going to enjoy? Let's not try to damage any more than we have to.

Tule/Bah De Bah

When you pull it out from the water, there's lots of white roots. It's good for lots of things. There's lots of them over in Pine Valley. Soak them in water. Take a bath in it. It's good for rheumatism and arthritis. It's all over the country, wherever there is dampness in the ground. Even the Chinese have these. If you have toothache or any kind of ache in your stomach, chew that and it will numb it for you right now, within five minutes. Any kind of ache. If you mash it up and put it on your leg or your arm, it will numb it for you. Harvest it in the spring of the year. Look for the yellow and white flowers. Animals take the leaf off right away. People can too. Take the green part for making salad. It tastes kinda sweet. If you don't harvest it in April, you'll never find it again.

Turkey Foot (Bluestem Grass)

It's a root that grows in California, Nevada, Wyoming, Montana, South and North Dakota. It has a white flower, stands almost five feet high. But it has a deep root, maybe five feet deep, and grows in dry ground. It's good for swelling and for colds. Put it in a bath to clean your skin and open up your pores. You can cook with it too.

7 | The Nature Way

From the beginning of life, this Mother Earth was a red ball. Rocks were melted together. They continued to melt together because the Earth is in space, and just like a meteorite, it was hot at one time. When it was hot, what kind of life was there when it was melting together? There was no water, there was nothing until the water formed on this Earth of ours and cooled it off, starting a new life, a different kind of life to what we've got now. The life that was planted here was healthy 'cause they were put here for a reason. The life began from those melted rocks. We come from within the rock itself, and today you see those things. There's a plant in a solid rock, how did it start? It cracks the rock, the roots get in there and continue to grow.

There's life within that rock. It's got a voice like we do, it sings songs like we do, and most of the people can hear those things. Most of the time the people see the rocks move, what moves them? There's a spirit there. It's hard to understand those things have been happening for a long time.

The plant life drinks water like we do, eats food like we do, breathes air like we do. We think a plant life just naturally grows by itself, but it doesn't. It has to have songs, it has to have a word from us to keep it moving. Those are the reasons why the wind sings songs to them, talks to them, and our job is to tell the plant to keep their life healthy and strong so some day when we use them, they can heal us.

All the animal life, when you look at them, this is what they do. You see little creatures rely on flowers because they enjoy them, and it was put there for them to use just like us. We are going to have to relearn those things again in order for us to really understand why all the living things are on this planet. We're all put here together, we cannot let one plant die out thinking it's going to replace it with another. Our plant life throughout the world is dying out because we forgot how to pray for them, to ask for their life to continue. Your forefathers and my forefathers have done those things, they worked with the Nature. That's how they survived.

During the full moon the plant life drinks lots of water because the Nature brings the water to the surface for them to drink. Early in the morning, the dew on the plants was put here to do those things. Man didn't create those things because man didn't know, and today we're still in the darkness about those things, but we're saying somebody created it. If there was such a thing as that, we would continue to create a lot of different things, but we can't. We have to rely on Nature, but we're trying to change the way Nature put things here. We're trying to change the Nature to our way, but it's not working—it never will work.

Sometimes we, the people, don't realize all the living things out there have got a voice, they've got a spirit like we do. The plant life is something that we don't understand, how important it is to see flowers on all the different kinds of plants. They were put here for us to use, but we, the people, have to ask them to continue to support us and we must support them. All the life on this Earth today has to take care of each other. Those are the reasons why my people used to tell me, "whenever you take a life of all different things, make sure you tell them why you're taking their life. Even if it's a plant, it understands you, it can work with you if you ask. When you ask those things to take care of you, it can take care of you."

In order for us to do those things, we have to continue to ask the Nature to work with us the best way it can. Those are the reasons why I was taught not to destroy things but make sure you work with them, because they were put here for a reason just like we are. We are put on this Mother Earth for a reason. We didn't just come here not knowing what we're supposed to be doing. We're supposed to know from the beginning of our life why the life was put here, just like the plant life I was talking about. It had to be here and continue its life. It renews itself just like we do. We've got a Mother and we've got a Dad. A plant life is the same way, there's no difference. It has to have clean food, it has to have clean air, just like we do.

Just like the seed when you put it in the ground, it will develop into something great, maybe food, a tree, or shade. It can be a beautiful thing for us to use.

So when you see a tree, it was put here for a lot of reasons: to beautify the Mother, for the birds to use so they will build their nest in the tree, and the animal life uses the tree to rub itself against it. And then we sit under a tree to get away from the sun and to get in the shade. Sometimes when you don't feel good, you lean up against a tree. That tree can heal you, it can give you strength, it can give you energy. The Nature has said to the trees, "When your life ends, that's not the end of your life. You are going to continue to do your work even if you are dead, you are still going to be used as lumber for fire."

It can be used for a lot of different things, that tree, so its life never ends, it continuously goes on. Each year it grows older. We can tell a tree's life from how long it's been on this Earth. We know it drinks water because it's got water contained in it. We know it eats food of some kind. The food that you eat today came from a seed. Same with us. We, the human race, came from a seed, but somebody has to take care of us. Our mommy is very important. Man is a seed carrier, he plants the seed. Same with the Nature, it does the same thing, no difference. Today all of us, all the living things, come from a seed on this planet of ours. Those are the reasons why the Mother Earth takes care of us, because we have to have a mommy to take care of us. Look what it's given us for millions of years. It gives us water, clean water. It gives us healing water, what we call mineral water. It gives us clean air so that we can continue to breathe. It gives us a lot of different things.

Deer was put here on this Mother Earth with us. The deer has said to us from the beginning, "I'm here for you if you're ever hungry. I'm here to feed you, but before you take my life make sure you tell me why you're taking my life. If you take my life, if you ask me to continue, I'll continue, I'll be waiting for you at the same place where you took my life. I'm here for you, but make sure when you do take my life, use every bit of me, don't throw me around. That way I'll appreciate my life and you'll appreciate me."

Those are the things we were told, and we have to continue to do those things. We had to get that message out there. We have to continue to tell this to our young generation, generation after generation, in order for their life to continue. The animal life have said to us, "if you don't appreciate me living here with you on this Earth, I can disappear."

So we, as Native people, see that—we see what's happening. We're taking some things' life without even telling them why we're taking their life. Those are the reasons why they're disappearing.

The Laws of Nature

The plants, the animals, the birds have all got rules and regulations that they go by. They go south in the fall of the year, where it's warmer, just like the Indian people used to do. They go north to the higher mountains in the summertime, when it's hotter.

Let me explain to you just a very little bit about how Nature changes the animal life. Certain times of the year the bird life has different kinds of feathers, warmer feathers for the winter, cooler feathers for the summer. Animals' fur coats are thicker in the wintertime than they are in the summer. Take the example of the snowshoe rabbit. In the middle of the winter, in January, their fur turns white and their eyes turn red so they don't get snow blind from the snowflakes. And then, in February/March, he gets a bigger foot. When the snow is slushy, he can run on top of the snow and outrun a predator. In the summertime they turn gray. Weasels do the same thing. In the summertime they're brown, in the wintertime, when the snow's on the ground, he's totally white. So how did he know when to change? The Nature is the one that changes those things.

We must think about it, how important those creatures are. They're showing us what they can do and how they can survive. We should be watching how the Nature works. A lot of things work differently from each other, but they've all got rules and regulations they have to follow. This is why my people don't hunt those animals until certain times of the year, when the rules and regulations of Nature told us to take their life. Like deer, for example. Certain times of the year their meat is tough, and certain times of the year they are tender. This is what we watch. Same with birds. Certain kinds of birds were put here for them to get tender, or sometimes, when they're tough, they don't have a good taste or they taste tough.

When I was very young, my people, in the spring of the year, like February and March, would say that this is when the sagehen would get fat. They're there for us to take their life. We didn't have any guns, no gunpowder. You had to use a bow and arrow, the only weapon we had, or sometimes somebody would trap them with a string made out of a cord or the backbone of an animal. This is why my people always tried their best to continuously tell us what we are going to expect from the Earth itself. They kept telling us over and over, "Make sure you take care of them, ask them to continue their life, because they are the things you are going to survive on. If you don't take care of them, someday you're going to go hungry."

Day and night they talked to us, it seemed to me, because when I was young, I remember my grandma used to be talking when I'd go to sleep at night, and in the morning when I'd wake up, she was still talking. I guess she tried to pound it into my head what it was I had to go through, what I had to appreciate. The Nature put the medicine out there for us to use. It's there, if we take care of it, if we sing to it, talk to it, and tell it the reason why we're taking its life, then it's working with us. This is why the Native people throughout the country have their ceremonies. They get together and have their dances, praying from early in the morning before sunrise until noon.

Singing Songs to Nature

In the morning I sing songs like the birds. The birds sing songs early in the mornings until the sun comes up. Then they start eating. Our forefathers used to do the same thing.

When I was young, one guy used to ride a white horse and go around the Indian camp telling people, "you'd better get up and do your morning prayer," and the people would get into a big circle and pray for all the living things to continue their life. First thing they used to tell the sun to continue to shine upon the Earth, to warm everything and wake up everything. They had a bucket of water sitting there, and the spiritual man, he would walk up to the water and pray to that water and sprinkle it on the ground and ask the people to walk up there and do the same thing. A lot of people prayed to the water, and they sprinkled themselves or they washed their face and put water in their hands. Same with the air, they used to say good things to the air, how wonderful that air is and how wonderful everything is. They asked the grass to continue to grow for all the animal life to survive on.

Singing songs is very important, not only for Native people, but for all people. All the creatures that roam this Earth sing songs, because songs were put here by the Nature so that we can enjoy them together. Always remember when somebody doesn't feel good, sing them a song to make them feel better. We've all been taught that, but we didn't pass the knowledge on. We thought it was going to take care of itself. It's not going to take care of itself. We're the ones that are going to have to really do what we can, to ask the Nature to give us a lending hand and give us something to survive on.

Now we are witnessing our Mother trying to get away from us. She is going to give up on us one of these days. We've already begun to see the waves of the ocean are getting higher, the heat waves are getting hotter, the sun is putting radioactive rays on us, the wind is not pure to breathe. We're the ones that are causing these things. Our water is drying up and we, the people, are not getting along with each other. We're disgusted with life, we're disgusted with the world. We don't understand why.

Without this world, remember, you're not going to be able to live. Without the healing power of Nature, you won't be able to survive.

I know when we talk about water, that water is a very important part of our life because we're part of that water. When the Native people go up into the hills to wherever there's a spring, they're always talking to it, cleaning it, and singing to it so that it continuously flows. Today we see our water is disappearing from us because we didn't appreciate it, not like our forefathers. Our forefathers used to sing songs, talk to the water, and be glad that they had clean water before they even touched it, before they even took a drink out of it.

Today some of the things that we used to survive on are gone, like our birds. The birds that were put here by Nature here in Shoshone country are not here anymore. We don't have many sagehens left. Sagehens are what our forefathers have survived upon for many years. We have a ceremony for them and they have a ceremony for themselves. Every February/March the sagehen has their ceremony. They get together and sing their songs, talk to each other, and this is when they mate. They have never forgotten, but we're the ones that forgot, and today we miss those things that were put here with us.

Those are the reasons why I'm trying today to talk about it, so we can all understand where our medicine comes from. Let's think back a few thousand years, when there was no modern medicine on this Earth. Our medicine was provided by the Nature itself. This is something that we've been taught from the beginning of our life, but the younger generation today are lost because they don't know what to say, when to say those things, but our forefathers tried to tell us the certain time of year, certain time of the month they had to be talked to so they would understand what we're saying, why we appreciate them, and so forth. Today we're realizing that we're losing everything because we never appreciated what was put out there for us to use. Our songs are connected to all of those things. Singing our songs and teaching our songs is very important. For many, many years the Nature has given us songs to work with. Different kinds of songs about different kinds of things. If you are given a song for you to use, that's your song. In different parts of the country we've got different ways of singing. Let's continuously learn our songs so that we can continue to use them, teach them, and pass the knowledge on. We have to understand how our people have survived for thousands and thousands of years, and today that knowledge is really lost because we never passed it down from one generation to another. We quit talking about those things. We need our medicine today, we need our food of all different kinds.

Power to Work with Nature

At one time the Native people were given the power to work with the clouds, the water, animals, birds, and all the living things.

When I was young, on 4th July people had horse races, foot races, all different kinds of races. I have seen people bet on whether a horse can outrun a man or either a man can outrun a horse. It was hard to believe that a man could outrun a horse, because a horse has four legs but a human has only got two legs. I have seen a middle-aged Indian man, in his forties, race against a horse. Of course from the beginning of the race the horse ran away from the Indian, who was running on foot, and left him behind. They had to go over a mountain for three miles, pick up a rag at the other end, and then back to the beginning. The horse was in the lead going toward the top of this hill. Before they got to the top, the man was there on foot right alongside the horse. Going down the hill, that part I didn't see, but I was told a human can outrun a horse down the hill because he understands the shape of the land. But a horse had to be careful because of rocks and badger holes. The guy that was riding the horse, he had to make sure he held on tight to the horse because he didn't have a saddle, it was bare. Going over the hill, coming back to the beginning of the race, the man on foot was over the top of this mountain and half way down before the horse got up there to the top from the other side. The horse didn't do much good. But the man he worked with the Nature, he worked with the clouds, he moved with them, so he could run really fast.

I have also seen not too long ago in Duckwater, Nevada, where an Indian doctor walked up to an eagle who was sitting down alongside the road and petted him.

That's how the Nature works, that's how the Nature gives the power to certain people.

Many years ago I worked with an Indian doctor, his name was Horace Duckeye. He was from the Four Corners area in the Southwest, and he was a powerful man. I have seen him work on many people who had different kinds of sickness. One time I remember, in Battle Mountain, he worked on a young lady who had cancer in her legs from the hip on down. He cut her open with his finger. That kind of power people used to have long ago. When he cut her leg open, he scraped that bone. There was a sickness on her bone. So he scraped that off with his finger, and when he got through, he put his hand over it and ran his hand over where he cut. You couldn't see where that cut had been. It didn't leave any mark. That's the kind of power the Native people had because it was gifted from Nature itself. I think some people still have that kind of power today.

When I was a young boy, I saw my uncle doctor a person that had been dead for awhile. His family knew he was dead, but they asked my uncle to doctor this person. All night long my uncle doctored the dead man, and his spirit told my uncle that he had gone through a black tunnel toward the north. That's where we all go when our spirit leaves our body. This person's spirit told my uncle to remove a can outside the log cabin where he was doing his doctoring. There was an old five-gallon coffee can lying outside, and I heard the spirit say to my uncle that he had to remove this can before he could return into his body. When the spirit came in, not through the door but through the walls of the log cabin, everybody saw this dead person start to move his hand. I think everybody was surprised, some people started crying, and my uncle showed us where he had to peel off the brown stuff on this spirit of the man. The spirit looks like a pine nut, but it floats around like a feather. When my uncle put this spirit back into him, he started to move his head and see what was going on. First thing he asked, as I remember, was "why are we doing this?"

My uncle told me that he had to go through this black tunnel to the spirit world, and the spirit didn't want to come back through the tunnel. But my uncle kept begging him, and finally they came back together through the tunnel.

I have also seen another Indian doctor, Willy Blackeye from Duckwater, Nevada, heal the spirit of a young girl that was in a car wreck near Currant Creek, Nevada. She was in a coma for three months. They took her to San Francisco and Salt Lake, but they could never get her out of this coma, until the time Willy Blackeye worked on her and brought her spirit back to her body.

There were a lot of Indian doctors at that time throughout the country. Working with Nature is a very important part of our life because the Nature chose our spiritual people to doctor us, to keep us alive, and tried to teach us not to do bad things, but do good things for each other.

I "Died" Two Times

Way back in 1928, when I was eight years old, a horse fell on me and knocked me out, early in the morning when me and my uncle were taking the cattle out from Blackfoot, Idaho, up into the hills. We were going over a river, and there was a gate going into another field, and one of the cows got into this field. This gate was closed and I was on a horse. I tried to go through this gate by opening it while I was still on my horse, and I knocked the top part of this gate down, but the lower part of it was still hanging on. I tried to force this horse to go over the wire gate. He stepped over it, but then he reared back and got caught and fell backward on me, and this is when I got knocked out. It was in the morning, the sun was up high. When I came to, the sun was setting and my uncle was doctoring me. He said I had been unconscious all day and that I had stopped breathing. I thought it was still morning, but my uncle and the other cowboys wrapped me in blankets and took me to Pocatello General Hospital, where I stayed for a few days.

The second time I almost died was in Battle Mountain, Nevada, when I was in my thirties. I lost a lot of blood when I fell off my horse and cut my arm. I passed out, started to go north. My spirit went toward the foothills, toward Midas, Nevada. There's a spring that comes out of the rocks up high and runs down from there. Everything looked so beautiful, and when I was at this little creek, I saw two little fawns on the other side. I kneeled down to drink water, but I looked at these two fawns. On the right side of myself there was a bird, a beautiful-looking bird, he was red, yellow, and blue. Then the two fawns came across that little creek and started to go back toward Battle Mountain, and this is when the bird started to follow them. I started to follow the bird and the fawns. I tried to touch them and grab them, but they were a little bit out of my reach. When I came to, I was lying in my house and there were a lot of people crying. The very first thing I asked was, "Why are you guys crying? What's happening?" The doctor at that time was there from Battle Mountain, he was an old doctor. He told me, "you've been dead for twenty minutes, you didn't have any life in you at all." That's all he told me. He said it was a miracle that I had come back to life. This is what I've been through. I guess I experienced it two different times in my time. There are a lot of people out there that have been through the same thing as I have. People should really understand that if you are really good to Nature, you can be taken care of by Nature and it can protect you whatever happens to you.

Death

My grandmother told me when I was very young that before you die, you have to make up your mind what you want to be when you return to Earth. Whether you want to be a bird, an animal, a rock, or a plant, make up your mind, so when you pass on you know right from the beginning where you're going and what you're going to be.

Our way of putting away a dead body is totally different from the European way of burying the dead. Let's think back a few thousand years ago, we didn't have any shovels, we didn't have any picks, we didn't have any crowbars to dig the ground. We knew the badger could dig a hole if there is a shallow place, and they can smell your body. They can dig you up. Those are the reasons why the Native people buried a dead body in the rocks, so the badger and other animal life couldn't dig them up. They put the body in with sagebrush and with all different kinds of herbs. They sing songs, they sing your song, they remind everyone what you used to say and what you used to do. This is what they talk about before they put you into your resting area. For the next three years they always go back to where they have put you. If you've got a family, they go over there for the first three years at the same time, same place. Who have you left behind, who left you behind? These things are all mentioned, so that way everybody knows who your relatives are.

Mysteries of Nature

My grandma used to talk about how there were different colors of Native people here on this Earth. There were dark people, pretty dark like black people but they were from this part of the continent. And there were yellow people. There are pinto people, who have white and red spots all over their body. I knew a guy that was pinto, he was an Indian man with white spots all over his body and two eyes that were different colors to each other. I have seen people that are blue and black in color. This is something that is really hard to believe today, but there are still red people, blue people, and purple people out there in the jungles of South America.

The same thing with hair color. Hair color was different. When I was a young boy in the 1920s, I saw a lot of Shoshone women that had red hair. They were dark skinned, but they had red hair. I thought they were from a different world, but I was told there are all different colors of people on this Earth with different hair colors and different skin colors.

Everything on this Earth comes in different shapes, sizes, colors. This is Nature, so we also are part of the Nature. We're not all the same.

Another thing that the Nature has put out there that few of us have seen or heard are water babies. They live in fresh-water springs and they cry like little babies. I have seen three of them myself, one in Duckwater, Nevada, one in Owyhee, Nevada, and one in Snake River, Idaho, but I have never seen their faces. I have heard them crying in Bruneau Canyon, Idaho. They look like a small child around three years old, but their bones are fully developed. They don't wear any clothes, they're naked. This is the same thing as Earth babies. A lot of people have seen them, a lot of people have heard about them, but have never seen them. They have thrown a rock behind me or before me when I'm roaming around the country. They're little people, stone people as I call them.

Not too long ago I heard a lot of Shoshone people talk about a flying wolf that they had seen in Duckwater, Fort Hall, and parts of Montana. They said the flying wolf would be attracted to a campfire in the evening, or if it heard a baby crying. The people would hide their kids and put out their fire, because the flying wolf would steal the babies and eat them. Not too long ago, in the early 1940s, people in Duckwater heard a flying wolf coming from Ely, over Mount Hamilton. Some people were told that a sheepherder had found a skeleton of a wing of a flying wolf near Sand Springs, between Duckwater and Eureka. It had a three-feet wingspread. Those are the things our forefathers have seen and heard, but in our modern days we have never seen something like that, but we will as the time goes on. Because those things that were here before on this part of the world are going to be seen again by us in the near future.

The Native people throughout the country and the people around the world believed at one time that when a woman is on her moon or period, her blood is life, life given by the Nature. You see an animal roaming out there by itself away from the herd, then that female is on her moon. When you see other animals doing the same thing, then they're on their moon. This is why we used to bleed a man quarterly, every three months, in order to get that blood out of him so that he could feel fresh again instead of feeling run down. This is how important that blood is.

Take a tree, for example. On the full moon all the trees are heavier, because this is when they bring the water clear to the top of their trunk. If you cut a tree down on the full moon, it will be heavier than at any other time because it's got liquid in it. This is when the Native people say the tree is sucking the mommy's blood into it. The mommy's blood is water. The moon has a lot to do with life. Every month there's a full moon, and the moon is either going up or coming down. This is what our forefathers have followed for many, many years. Certain phases of the moon, you plant your seeds for different things. Certain times of the month we are heavier because we've got life-giving blood. Anytime when you cut yourself on the full moon, you bleed more.

This is why the Native people around the world really protected themselves and made sure they didn't harm anybody else. When a woman is on her moon, she can hurt another woman or hurt a man because, if she comes into contact with someone that's weak or sick, she can make them even weaker. They begin to feel lousy and more run down because the blood of a woman is strong toward you, especially when they're near you. You can feel it and you can smell it.

This is why my people had moon lodges away from the house, because we didn't want everybody to feel heavy and lazy. When a girl turned into a woman, then every month she had to go out there into the moon lodge and cook for herself. Today throughout the world the moon lodge is still being used by some people, but not many.

A woman on her moon could only use her own plate and her own cup, because our people always used to say, "when you're on your moon, don't cook for anybody, don't mess around with washing dishes."

If you use someone else's dishes, then you make people heavier than what they are or lazier or even sick.

But today we're living in a modern world. Like our toilets. We can only use one toilet today in a household. But what are we doing with our water? We're mixing it up with a women's blood, and the life is stronger than the water itself. So it dries the water up.

When a woman is on her moon, it means she's strong, her blood is strong, she's a life giver, and she gives blood to all of us. The air that she breathes, the life within her body relies on that.

It's important to think and realize these things yourself. How do you feel when a woman on their moon comes near you? You can feel it because you begin to not have a good feeling and not have much strength. This is why I always warn a woman on her moon to never jump across a creek, because it damages the spirit of that water. I have seen this time and time again, when a woman on her moon goes across or jumps over a creek, then the water begins to get heavier. The ripple will tell you it's not doing what it was doing before. These things my people talked about a long time ago, and they are still important today. So I'm saying to you, think about your moon and how important it is. If it wasn't for that blood of a woman, we wouldn't be here, so think about how important a woman is and how that blood she gives us keeps us as a human race alive and strong.

Catching Fish/Bengwi-Yickwi

At one time we didn't have fishhooks and we didn't have lines, so we used a basket which we would hold above a waterfall.

You watch a bear and see what he does. A bear goes to a waterfall and makes sure he stands above it, because when the fish jump up from the water to go upstream, then this is when the bear catches it.

The basket that the Native people made was about five feet long. The little fish will go through the basket, but it will catch the big fish. This is how our people used to catch fish.

There's another way of catching fish, and that's by using a long pole with arrowheads on the end of it. You can stab them, but you had to stand in the water or near the water. The waterfall was usually better, because then we followed the Nature Way and watched what the bear did.

Throughout the country the Native people knew where to go at certain times of the year. They didn't catch fish at anytime, they had to have seasons. At certain times of the year the fish are fat, and at certain times of the year they're saving all of their blood for the younger fish to be born. That's their moon blood. That's how important that moon circle is.

Natural Living

The wigwam, or the tepee as we call it nowadays, is now made with cloth. It used to be covered with different animal hides like buffalo skin, deerskin, and antelope skin. Even when I was a young boy, wigwams were covered with cloth and blankets. This is how we survived during the winter months in the wigwam. There would be about six to eight people living in there. In the modern wigwams there was often a stovepipe sticking out from the middle of it. Long ago it never had those things, never had an opening on the top for smoke, because a wigwam at that time was made out of sagebrush.

We traveled from one place to the other. We'd pick a place where there was a lot of sage or wherever there were a lot of trees. We'd make a shelter out of them, and this is what we call the wickiup. We didn't have animals, so we had to carry all of our possessions ourselves. The skins and blankets were too heavy to carry from one place to the other, which is why we built the wickiup from sagebrush. We made a shelter out of them, so that no animal could come into them. At that time there was a lot of animal life that would disturb people.

Everything was done outside, like our cooking. If it was raining, we made sure there was an overhang of a rock that we could cook under. Everything we ate had to be dried. We made everything dry by the sun.

Today, when we see pictures of wigwams and when we talk about those things, it's very hard for people to understand how we had to struggle in order to survive. We had to rely on the Nature. It provided us with the sagebrush and the trees.

In Grass Valley, Nevada, there used to be an Indian ranch. There's a frame there that was built a long time ago to keep the meat cool. Even in the hot days, a gunnysack was used around this frame. When the wind blows, it can really keep meat cool during the night and during the day because of that gunnysack. When you wet the gunnysack and when the breeze is going through it, it acts the same as a modern water cooler or swamp cooler. It keeps things cool. It's got a fresh-water spring running underneath it, and above there used to be a wooden pipe that came through the top of this frame. This is how the Indian people saved their meat for months at a time. This place is in the middle of nowhere, so the people had to rely on Nature. This was built way before any electricity was ever developed, but still the people knew how things worked.

Right next to this is a stone house that was also built by the Indian people. During the summer months, when it's hot, the stone house is cool. During the winter months, when it's cold, the stone house keeps warm. All that's left now is the framework. The roof has burned down. It had a dirt floor, the kind of dirt that water doesn't go through. You see that throughout the country. Some places the water doesn't soak through clay. It'll run off it, but it won't wash it away, it gets solid and hard. This is why the Native people have looked for dry lake beds where there's clay.

We, the Native people, survived on this land. We had to really take care of each other in order for us to survive. At one time we were concerned about each other because life was important to us. We always had something to give to the needy, we gave them a lending hand. We were concerned about life. We made things out of different hides and feathers. In order for us to trade, we had to go many, many miles to meet with different bands in different parts. We traded things, and we enjoyed meeting each other.

Those are the reasons why throughout the country our forefathers knew where there was clean water and clean food. The important part of the whole thing was that we had scouts. A scout was a man who went out to find food and a good campsite and then came back to report to the women's committee. At one time, the women were the leaders of all the different tribes. They told the men scouts to go and see where they're going to camp, where is the food, where is there a nice place with a spring. Then the women would make the final decision as to where the tribe would camp and told the men, "you have to gather wood and bring in the food, the game of different kinds." The women would go out and collect different kinds of seeds and berries.

Everything's got a female and a male on this Mother Earth, I don't care what it is. Rocks have a female, plants have a female, water has a female. Females are the ones that give us life, and a human female is the one that brings life onto this Earth. The man is just the provider, and the woman is the giver of life. We see throughout the world that the woman takes care of the young life that's come up on this Earth, and she makes sure she teaches them the right things. You see an animal teaching their young how to survive and what to do. This is something that they had to follow from generation to generation. Most of you have seen a duck crossing a road or a river. The mommy is in the lead and the little ones follow her. Same with any other animal, the mommy always takes the lead and the little ones follow. Same with the plant life, the one big one and the little ones around it.

When we see those things happening, then you can understand how Nature works.

When the women did decide where they were going or what they were going to do, the men always let the women make the final decision. The women provided food for us, they kept us in peace. At one time I was told, "don't misuse a woman, but take care of them in order for them to take care of you. You've got to be the one to show them how important they are."

This is why today a women's council is a very important thing that women have to organize, to gather themselves together and start the movement the way it should be, not like the corrupt way of living that we've got now. Women have got a better voice, they're the peacekeepers, they're the life givers, they're the teachers. Let's keep them strong and healthy as much as we can.

PART IV

Surviving in the Modern World

8 | Protecting Nature

For many years we have been trying to put a stop to nuclear testing at the Nevada Test Site, because we knew it was going to create problems. When they test a bomb, the radiation gets into the air, it moves across the world. But the DOE (the Department of Energy) keeps telling us the same thing over and over: "It's not that dangerous."

They keep saying it's not that dangerous, but our people are continuing to die from cancer caused by radiation. This radiation has caused all different kinds of sickness, especially cancer. You get bone disease when radiation comes up from the bottom of your feet. Long ago, my people roamed with no shoes. That's why the first thing to do when you sit down is to wash your feet. Even animals will put their feet in different water.

I think everybody knows cancer is spreading all over the world. The DOE knows it, but they're telling people a lie.

At the Nevada Test Site, the DOE is now telling people that when the wind was blowing northeast, then this is when they set the nuclear bombs off in the 1950s and 1960s. They made sure the wind was not blowing toward the coast, or toward the big cities like Los Angeles and Las Vegas. When the wind was blowing northeast through Utah, many of the Native people throughout the reservations were hurt, but the DOE kept repeating the same thing over and over, that "we are going to help you." They were going to set up some kind of program to have us checked and treated, but so far it's never been done.

In 1953 they tested many nuclear bombs that carried a lot of radiation downwind over southern Utah. About two thousand sheep were affected by the radiation, most of them dying within a short time.[1]

It also crippled many people's horses and chickens. Some of the chickens, their growth was awful to see. They became huge, they couldn't move around too much, and the same thing with the people in St. George, Utah, it crippled them. Many, many people today are still suffering on account of this.

Bombs are something we, the Native people, don't appreciate because they are there to wipe out the life of all the living things. We, the people, have been put here by the Creator to take care of the Mother Earth, the water, the air. The Creator is the one that put this water here for us to use, not only us, but all the living things. A lot of my people have died. A lot of other people have died, a lot of animals died, a lot of birds died, all the plant life has died. Most of the food that my people have survived on for thousands of years has disappeared. The nuclear bombs have killed them. It killed the medicine that we used to use for different kinds of sickness. When they died, we became lost. We all began to go to the pharmacist. The Nature has given up on us, you see that today. Look at our water today throughout the world. Why are we buying water, when the Nature put this water here on this Earth for all the living things to survive on? Everything drinks that water, everything uses it in a way to keep it clean. This is what we're supposed to be doing, praying for that water, asking that water spirit to continue to be strong and clean. This is what my forefathers have done, and your forefathers have done the same thing. We were all concerned about those things at one time. Until somebody said, "you don't have to do that, it's nature, it'll come by itself." It does come all right, contaminated with all kinds of chemicals and radiation. You have to think about the plant life, the animal life, the bird life. All the creatures that survive on water, their water's getting contaminated with chemicals, and it's us doing the damage.

We're throwing chemicals out there on the ground. From the ground it goes right into our water table. Our water table is getting so bad that now we have begun to tell each other, "I don't want to drink this water, I'd rather drink bottled water." How many of you people can kneel down and take a drink from spring water? Most of us today are too scared to drink that water coming from the mountainside. Very few places today have got water that's usable coming out of the Earth.

So you buy water. This is what we're doing today. But very few people are going to benefit from this water very much longer, because we already see the water we're buying is dead, it doesn't have any life to it. Some day this bottled water is going to run out, and where are we going to go for water after that? When we think about these things, let's remind ourselves, our forefathers talked to the water, they talked to the air, they talked to the sun, they talked to the moon, they talked to the wind. This is why at one time the wind was gentle, it gave you a lot of fresh air, but when we don't talk to it, it creates problems for us. It picks up the dust, all the chemicals, all the garbage, all the waste we put onto the land. It picks it up and brings it back to us through the wind. And we have to breathe those things. It blocks up our lungs, and then we don't feel good. Some creatures die from the wind and the chemicals and pollution that we're putting out there. We're the ones creating problems for ourselves and for all the living things. The animal life today is suffering because their food is disappearing, because we put too much radiation out there. All you see of an animal today is alongside the road surviving off our trash. What we've been throwing out is going into a trash can, we thought, but what we are really doing is dirtying our Mother Earth. The disease starts from this. This is where the radiation cancers begin from, from the radiation that we throw out there on the ground. This is what we've been trying to tell the DOE, but they're not listening. All they're doing is taking more life from the face of this Earth. Maybe they were put here to do those things. They don't have any feelings for the Mother Earth that provides them with food, provides them with water, and provides them with air. They're not thinking about their grandchildren and their grandchildren's children, all the way down the line. They just want to destroy.

If they say radiation's not dangerous, why are they shipping it throughout the country? If it's not dangerous, why don't they leave it where it's at? Are they telling the truth? I know they're not. I hope someday they are going to start telling the public the truth and not continue to say that radiation is not dangerous. If it wasn't dangerous, there'd be more lives on this planet of ours. But the young people are suffering today, they're dying by the thousands. In my travels throughout the country I have seen a lot of young lives born without parts of their body. This is wrong. When you see a life, it's just a vegetable, it doesn't have any life in it at all. It shouldn't be that way. Radiation is something we can't feel, we can't see, we can't smell until it affects us. It's dangerous stuff that somebody is messing around with. I hope someday they'll realize this if they want to continue to live on this planet. Maybe they're thinking about moving onto other planets. I would wish them good luck, they can move on and leave this Earth for us to survive on.

They say the nuclear power is cheap, but that's not so. It's a dangerous power, it continuously takes the life of all the living things on this planet. A lot of creatures that rely on Nature want it clean and healthy.

Today throughout the country all the fish life in the water has begun to die out, all kinds of life in the oceans have died. Most of the fish throughout the world have got sore spots on them. There's a lot of life on the shorelines of the oceans today dying by the millions. Why are we doing all of this damage to the creatures? When are we, the human race, going to wake up to the problem? When are we going to do something for them, or do we just think the Nature's going to take care of it? The Nature's going to take care of us all right, because we're already heading in that direction. All our lives are going to end. This is where we're heading, because the life we have today is corrupt. If we don't do something and help the Nature, everything's going to disappear from the face of the Earth.

If we are going to think about those things, we have to start doing it now. Those are the reasons why today our government is pushing to transport the nuclear waste over your highways, over your railroads, and out across the sea, because we never made a sound. We knew it was wrong, but we never said anything about it because we thought our government was protecting us. It's not protecting us, because we all see, we all read about these things. So far the trucks that are hauling this stuff are coming from the East, mostly from Oakridge, Tennessee, and going to the Nevada Test Site. There they dump the nuclear waste and go on to California to transport food. How much radiation is on that truck? Did anybody ever check that? Did the DOE ever warn us that these trucks have radiation on them and haul your water or your vegetables or whatever it hauls and takes it back to your supermarkets? And you go to your supermarkets and buy these things. Did you ever realize how much radiation is in all of this? Today our government is telling us that we have to use radiation on our food. They say it preserves it a little bit longer. Myself, I know, because I've been in the giant supermarkets checking the radiation on the vegetables with my Geiger counter. It clicks the Geiger counter.

They're transporting nuclear waste, and it's leaking on the trucks, on the railroad, and on the sea. We're throwing nuclear rods into the sea. Are we trying to get rid of all the life in the water?

Now the government wants to dump high-level nuclear waste on the Goshute Shoshone Reservation in Skull Valley, Utah, sixty-five miles from Salt Lake City, because they control the land.[2] Skull Valley is already surrounded by other toxic dumps, and many of the people suffered from the Dugway Proving Grounds south of there, which has tested biological and chemical weapons and released these gases into the air. What effect does this have on the health of the Native people that's living there? If they dump high-level nuclear waste there, that radiation is going to be there for many thousands of years.[3]

WHEN I LOOK at all the different kinds of life on this Earth of ours that has begun to die out, I keep thinking to myself that someday we are going to wake up and start doing something, because we all see the news, we all read the paper, most of us. We've seen the news about a leaking nuclear-waste truck on the road or an accident on the road. When a big, huge accident happens with a nuclear-waste truck, then where do we go? Where do we get fresh, clean water and clean air? How far away from it are we going to go? How long are we going to be out there, away from wherever the accident happens?

You see the radiation's half-life is twenty-four thousand years.

This is how long it takes to break down in half. This is something not to fool with, but we're fooling with it. How long are we going to fool around with something that dangerous? How long is it going to be before we realize that we can't have something like this traveling on our highways?

If we are thinking about these things, let's ask questions about it to each other. This is how we can come together by talking about it. What can we do to protect the Earth, the water that we drink, the air that we breathe, if an accident happens? The radiation leaks out, then the wind will carry it over the land. If it spills onto the land, onto the Earth, then the rainwater's going to continue to take it down. What's left of the surface, the wind will come along and pick it up and put it out there with the land again.

Now we're all in this together. We're either going to have to keep this boat of ours floating or we can sink it together. This is where we're heading, and today I'm asking you people to really look at this and see what you can do with us. We are the people that are going to have to really start talking about it. I have asked you around the world and told the people that we can work together as one. We cannot be separated anymore. This is the trick that our government used on the Indian people. That's what they call "divide and conquer," and they're doing the same thing to you people today.

Today, look at your trees. Have you ever followed a truck that's hauling big timbers down the road? The trees have brown spots in the middle. Those are sick trees. We have clear-cut the forests throughout the world. When we start doing those things, then we say we are saving the new forests, the new trees, but that's not true. Today when you plant a tree, a young tree, that tree is not pure and strong. It's a weak tree, and besides that, when you don't have any protection on your soil, what does it do? When it rains, it washes the topsoil down to us where we're at. Same with radiation. The radiation up there on the hill, every time it rains, what does it do? It brings it down onto the soil. From the soil onto the flat where we're living.

Look at the little tiny creeks coming off the mountainside. We're throwing all kinds of trash into it, and the things that live in this water today don't appreciate that at all. Today when you look at city streets, people are throwing trash into the gutters and onto the highway. Then the wind picks up the trash and brings it right back to you. It gets into your lungs. Same with this water. Every time it rains, it washes our good-looking streets and puts it down our drains. Where does the drainage go? It goes into our Mother Earth, from our Mother Earth into your faucet, into your home, and into your body. Someday you're not going to be able to use that faucet water. It's already happening in some places. There's nothing clean anymore, all caused by human hands.

We're sending so many missiles into the air today, we're contaminating what's out there between the Earth, the sun, the moon, and the stars. We're putting chemicals out there in space. And today we've begun to say, hey, the sun is causing some kind of radiation on our skin. We've got so much skin cancer because we're not praying to the sun and thanking it for its life and asking it to protect us.

Yucca Mountain

Yucca Mountain in Nevada is a very important hill, but it's more like a rolling hill than a mountain.[4] The Native people have always said it's a moving hill, because it's got a caliche line right between it. They also say that this is a huge snake going north. From a distance you can see it move, and it's going to continue to move. It has been moving for the last million years.

The DOE wants to put high-grade nuclear rods in this rolling hill, thinking the caliche line is going to stop any water from going into the tunnel. They built a tunnel in the hill to store the nuclear high-grade rods, but we, the Native people, said, "It's not going to work because there's movement in that hill. It's a snake in there, it'll continue to move." Not only that, but half a mile or so away from this hill are seven volcanoes. People should realize how dangerous it is to put nuclear rods in this hill.

That rolling hill we have survived on for millions of years. We worked with it, it worked with us. But the DOE wants to destroy it by putting deadly nuclear rods into it, which will heat up the hill and heat up the water below it. Once the underground water contacts the nuclear rods, what is it going to do?

It's going to heat up and make steam, and then the pressure of the steam will make the hill blow and set off the volcanoes which are surrounding the hill. What chance does any life have after that happens? There'll be no life left. Maybe we will destroy our Earth by putting those things there.

When they bring these nuclear rods into Yucca Mountain, how far are they bringing it? If it's that dangerous bringing it to Nevada, why don't they keep it where it's at, where they made the nuclear power in the generators? Store it there instead of moving it around the country. That's going to create more problems by transporting it on the railroads or on the trucks.

The reason why the DOE wants to store the nuclear waste here is because it's on Indian land under the Ruby Valley Treaty in 1863. Under this treaty the U.S. government agreed they were going to take care of this land, but instead they're trying to poison this tiny, rolling hill. We know it's poison, they know it's poison, because right down the valley, a few miles south from Yucca Mountain, is Amargosa Valley. There's a dairy farm there that supplies milk to parts of California. The farmer there is saying that this nuclear waste is going to contaminate the water underneath the surface. Then his cows are going to drink that water and be affected by radiation. What is that going to do to that milk? The people in California are going to be drinking poisoned milk.

People around the world are talking about how dangerous this nuclear energy is. Let's unite ourselves together and say NO to nuclear energy. Our scientists can come up with cleaner energy, like wind power, solar power, and water power. They have developed a machine that will go around the moon, that will go around this Earth, a few thousand miles up. Why can't they develop something better than nuclear energy before we lose everything?

You are the people that can stand up for your rights, instead of letting somebody dictate to us and tell us nuclear energy is not that dangerous when we all see how dangerous it is.

Notes

1 | My Early Years

1. Stewart Indian School (originally called the Carson Indian School) opened in 1890 south of Carson City. It was originally molded on the army's Carlisle Indian School in Pennsylvania. Named after Nevada's first U.S. senator, William Morris Stewart, it was the first and only off-reservation boarding school in Nevada for American Indian children. Children from Nevada and throughout the West were forced to attend the Stewart Indian School up to high-school age. Students came from many tribes, including the Nevada-based Washoe and Paiute tribes, as well as the Hopi, Apache, Pima, Mohave, Walapai, Ute, Pipage, Coropah, and Tewa. The school was intended to teach basic trades and to assimilate young American Indians into mainstream American culture. The curriculum underwent major changes in the 1930s, with many aspects of Indian culture no longer suppressed. In later years, the Bureau of Indian Affairs encouraged schools such as Stewart to let students speak their Native languages and to promote classes in Native cultures. Stewart Indian School closed in 1980 and is now a school museum.

2 | Working for My People

1. There does not appear to be a written treaty between Chief Tutuwa and the federal government. According to federal agent Warren Wasson, who visited with Chief Tutuwa and his band in 1861, they negotiated an oral agreement of which Wasson has stated: "On the twentieth of December, six o'clock, A.M., I arrived at Reese River where I met the chief To-to-a, and about one hundred of his band. I had a very satisfactory interview with them. The chief assured me of his friendship for our Government, and that none of his band would, under any circumstances, molest the stage or telegraph lines, or any whites that might want to visit or reside in his country. He seemed to regret that there was any disturbance between the whites and Shoshone, and volunteered to go with me and assist in bringing about a settlement." Myron

Angel, *History of Nevada 1881, With Illustrations And Biographical Sketches Of Its Prominent Men And Pioneers* (Oakland: Thompson and West, 1881), 177–18. Nowhere in this agreement did Tutuwa sell or give away land rights to the U.S. government. However this agreement was never ratified by the U.S. Senate, so it was never recognized by the government as an official treaty.

2. *Broken Treaty at Battle Mountain* (1974), sixty-minute film narrated by Robert Redford. Producer and director, Joel L. Freeman. *To Protect Mother Earth* (1990), the sequel, is an account of the Western Shoshone Dann sisters' struggle with the U.S. government to retain control of their ancestral lands and end nuclear-bomb tests. Both films have won numerous awards.

3. "Nevada Indian Days: A Proclamation by Governor Miller," September 13, 1989, State of Nevada Executive Department, Nevada State Archives, Carson City.

4. Dagmar Thorpe is the granddaughter of Olympic gold medalist Jim Thorpe. She is from the Sac and Fox tribe of Missouri, the interim executive director of the Fund of the Four Directions, and the acclaimed author of several Native books. Deborah Harry is Northern Paiute from Pyramid Lake, Nevada. She is an activist and executive director of the Indigenous Peoples Council on Biocolonialism. Pearl Dann is a Western Shoshone grandmother.

3 | Mistreatment of the Native People

1. Gale Ontko, *Thunder over the Ochoco,* vol. 1, *The Gathering Storm* (Oregon: Maverick, 1993), 393–94.

2. Visit by Corbin Harney and Hobbe Havewah to Repatriation Office at Smithsonian National Museum of National History, Washington, D.C., July 11, 12, 1994.

3. Shoshone Mike was a nomadic man who refused to settle on a government reservation and instead lived off the land the old way as his ancestors had done. But he was not a solitary body; he traveled with his wife, three sons, and other members of the tribe. On January 1911 a cattle company in Nevada saw that some of its cattle was missing and sent four men to track them down. The four men disappeared, their dead bodies later discovered. Shoshone Mike and his band were suspected of the murders and the missing cattle because the white ranchers considered them wild and dangerous, although there was no evidence that Mike was guilty. A fifteen-thousand-dollar reward was put up for Mike and his band, which stirred up a group of angry local whites who set

out to track them down. They eventually found the Indians in Clover Valley, northeastern Nevada, opened fire, and killed Shoshone Mike and seven of his band.

4. On October 1, 1863, the Ruby Valley Treaty of Peace and Friendship was signed between the Western Shoshone Nation of Newe Sogobia and the United States of America. The treaty described the boundaries of Western Shoshone Country, comprising some 60 million acres extending from the Snake River in Idaho through Nevada into Southern California. The treaty did not grant ownership of any Shoshone lands to the U.S government, although it granted the United States certain rights-of-way, mining rights, and the right to establish towns and ranches in support of mining. Additionally, the treaty granted the president authority to establish permanent reservations for the Western Shoshone within their territory. The U.S. Senate ratified the treaty in 1866, and President Grant confirmed it in 1869.

On July 7, 2004, President Bush signed the "Western Shoshone Distribution Bill," which authorized a payoff of approximately fifteen cents per acre for 24 million acres of land that was supposed to have been protected by the 1863 treaty. The settlement, totalling approximately $145 million, was welcomed by some in the Shoshone community who thought they should accept the money because there was no chance of regaining the land. However, a majority of involved tribal councils, including the Western Shoshone National Council, strongly opposed the bill, arguing that their ancestral lands were too high a price to pay. Politicians justified the bill based on polls of Shoshone individuals rather than the various tribal councils. Massive opposition by numerous traditional people, human rights organizations, and thousands of individual citizens delayed numerous votes on the bill but were ultimately unable to stop its passage. As a result of this, in August 2005 the Western Shoshone filed an urgent action request with the United Nations Committee on the Elimination of Racial Discrimination (CERD), which resulted in a formal letter from CERD to the U.S. government. The letter asks the U.S. government to explain its violations of treaty rights and the rapid pace of development on Western Shoshone land. Pressure tactics used by the government have included the seizure of livestock and the assessment of alleged trespass fines by the Internal Revenue Service and private collection agencies.

The Western Shoshone took their human rights case to the United Nations in Geneva, Switzerland, and on March 10, 2006 CERD urged the United

States Government to "freeze," "desist," and "stop" actions being taken or threatened to be taken against the Western Shoshone peoples of the Western Shoshone Nation. In its decision, CERD stressed the "nature and urgency" of the Shoshone situation, informing the United States that it goes "well beyond" the normal reporting process and warrants immediate attention under CERD's Early Warning and Urgent Action Procedure. This monumental action challenges the U.S. government's assertion of federal ownership of nearly 90 percent of Western Shoshone lands, although there is yet no reply from the U.S. government (extracted from www.shundahai.org).

5. *Editor's Note:* At this point in the draft manuscript that he was reviewing, Mr. Harney added: "There were different places where my people lost their lives, like Skull Butte and Riddle, Idaho, down into Little Valley, where the river drops down. Juniper Mountain is on the west side of a canyon. About seventeen miles away is an old fort. On the north side of it used to be an old capitol. There's an old fort there. In about 1864 or thereabouts. Not too far from what they call Butte, Idaho, there's Bruneau River and 'We Go Home' Mountain. Another place was Attatosgoro, out of Elko. White Rock used to be an Indian camp. There was a good spring there. They took a bulldozer and piled everything up—bones and all. Made a film of it. Another place was Big Cave in Butte, Idaho, where about 1,100 people were slaughtered, thrown into a hole with iron balls on their legs. There's a lookout, a high peak. We call it Chinaman's Hat. Pretty steep going down into there. Lots of eagles there. About 1954 Boise University took a research group out there."

6. "In a Nutshell," U.S. Department of Agriculture Forest Service publication, 1983.

7. Brigham D. Madsen, *The Northern Shoshoni* (Idaho: Caxton Printers, 1980), 202–3. According to the *Encyclopedia Britannica*, 15th ed., s.v. "sun dance," however, "in 1883, acting on the advice of Bureau of Indian Affairs personnel, the U.S. secretary of the interior criminalized the Sun Dance. . . . The prohibition was renewed in 1904 and reversed in 1934."

4 | Travels Across Newe Land

1. In 1933 President Hoover declared Death Valley a National Monument, an act that resulted in the Timbisha Shoshone's having no legal status for their land. They were also informed by the Park Service that they could no longer hunt or camp in Death Valley or continue with their seasonal migration into

the mountains. Their once vast domain was now restricted to forty acres of land near Furnace Creek under Park Service control. Over time life gradually improved for the tribe, but it wasn't until 1983 that they became federally recognized and therefore eligible for funding for electricity, renovation on the adobe houses, paved roads, and improvements to their water system.

A major breakthrough came in 1994, when the federal government passed the California Desert Protection Act, which added 3.2 million acres of land to the existing Death Valley National Park. A condition of this act established 7,500 acres of land to the Timbisha, thus creating a Timbisha Shoshone Natural and Cultural Preservation Area.

November 1, 2000, saw the passing of the Timbisha Shoshone Homeland Act, which extended the Timbisha site at Furnace Creek from 40 acres to 300 acres, with the remaining 7,200 acres of land having the potential for housing, small business development, and cultural-resource protection.

Included within this is special access and use for the tribe of sacred sites, springs, and mesquite groves.

2. "Project Faultless," January 19, 1968, information taken from site visit by Corbin Harney, August 2000.

5 | Healing with Our Prayers

1. Horned toads are also called horned lizards. Fourteen species are currently recognized, eight of which are found within the continental United States (one reaches southern Canada), and six other little-known species are restricted to Mexico (one reaches Guatemala). These lizards are creatures of hot, dry, sandy environments and have very wide, flattened, toadlike bodies. The tail is short but broad at the base. In most species the back of the head and temples are crowned with a prominent row of sharp, pointed horns. The tail and sides are fringed with sharp spines. On some species the sides are adorned with a double fringe of spines. On the back there are rows of short, conical spines. The back and head are soft desert gray. The markings are in pastel shades of tan, brown, red, or yellow. The underparts are pale, yellowish gray. The overall colors are generally close to the predominant color of the soil. Color changes from light to dark (or reverse) can occur within a few minutes.

1. I have struggled to find the English translation for *toza*. One possible translation is Indian balsam, although this has yet to be confirmed.

2. Letter from Sir Jeffrey Amherst, commander in chief of the British forces to a subordinate, July 16, 1732; E. Wagner and Allen E. Steam, *The Effects of Smallpox on the Destiny of the Amerindian* (Boston: Bruce Humphries, 1945), 44–45.

8 | Protecting Nature

1. Janet Burton Seegmiller, "Nuclear Testing and the Downwinders," The History of Iron County, http://www.historytogo.utah.gov/nuctest.html.

2. Due to immense protest and opposition from grassroots tribal members of Ohngo Gaudadeh Devia (OGDA, Goshute for "Timber Setting Community"), of the Skull Valley Band of Goshute Shoshone, plans to dump nuclear waste on reservation land have been abandoned.

In an effort to protect tradition and the health and safety of the reservation's inhabitants, OGDA, directed by Margene Bullcreek, opposes the dump.

On September 7, 2006, the BIA and the Bureau of Land Management (BLM) each delivered a Record of Decision, opting to take "no action" on the plan to store forty thousand tons of high-level nuclear waste on the Skull Valley Goshute Reservation in Utah.

The Skull Valley Goshute Reservation is located approximately forty-five miles north of Salt Lake City, is near various earthquake zones, and is surrounded by various military aircraft and weapons testing grounds.

Private Fuel Storage (PFS), a "limited-liability" consortium of commercial nuclear utilities, wanted to temporarily store nuclear waste in Skull Valley until the nuclear-waste facility at Yucca Mountain, Nevada, is in operation.

On February 22, 2006, the Nuclear Regulatory Commission (NRC) granted a license to PFS for its proposed nuclear-waste dump even though approval was still pending from the BIA and the public-comment period from the BLM had not ended.

In January 2007 PFS appealed against the decisions made by the U.S. Department of the Interior, arguing that they still have the license granted by the NRC and an agreement with the Skull Valley Goshute tribe. Although the three-member executive committee of the Skull Valley Tribal Council accepted the deal with PFS in 1997, arguing that it would economically benefit the tribe, it has been actively opposed by many members of the Skull Valley Band of Goshutes, as well as by many Indigenous organizations throughout the country, and has already been turned down by six other American Indian tribes within the United States. In September 2001 a team of tribal members officially challenged the Skull Valley Tribal Council's executive committee for a leadership election that would impact the PFS deal. To this day the results of that election are still in dispute, demonstrating the lack of consensus on the reservation for a high-level nuclear dump as a development option.

Throughout the process, OGDA has filed contentions with the NRC, continues to engage allied organizations in opposition, and participates in lawsuits to oppose the dump. Also, Sammy Blackbear, with the support of the Environmental Justice Foundation, is engaged in legal actions that impact the validity of the PFS deal (extracted from www.shundahai.org).

3. *Editor's Note:* At this point in the draft manuscript that he was reviewing, Mr. Harney added, "In Skull Valley, there are three different kinds of mud to take care of radiation."

4. In the late 1970s government scientists began to study Yucca Mountain as a possible repository for nuclear waste, and since 1987 it has been the only site considered for 77,000 metric tons of spent nuclear fuel and radioactive waste. Ninety-eight percent of all the radioactive waste generated by U.S. nuclear reactors may soon be headed for the mountain. There is already more nuclear waste than the repository can hold, unless the 77,000-ton limit is raised. Reactor waste now sitting in pools of water around the country will fill Yucca Mountain's tunnels and leave room for less than one-third of the government's nuclear-defense waste, leaving 15,000 canisters of radioactive waste (7,500 metric tons) with no place to go. Commercial nuclear-power plants produce 2,000 tons of high-level waste per year, and by the time Yucca Mountain is full in 2035, there will be 42,000 tons of newly generated civilian waste at reactors around the country. The estimated cost of construction and maintenance of the facility for the first 100 years of operation is $58 billion. The waste is lethal for 10,000 years and dangerous for 250,000 years.

For years there has been continuous wrangling over legislation to authorize site approval and waste transport to Yucca Mountain, and congressional votes have been very close. Current DOE plans call for the highly radioactive nuclear waste to be encased in steel containers and buried deep in the mountain. Since the canisters will last for 1,000 years at most, the dryness of the mountain will have to guarantee against leakage and migration, an idea that environmentalists and many scientists say is a flawed and dangerous assumption. Surface water percolates into the mountain and will carry radioactive particles into the water table and render it toxic. This water table currently supplies water to local communities and farming regions that produce milk and other food products for the entire country.

In February 2002 the Bush administration formally recommended construction of the waste dump. As is permitted in the federal law governing the location of America's nuclear-waste repository, Nevada's governor vetoed the Bush recommendation, but he was overridden by the House of Representatives (306–117) and Senate (60–39).

President Bush signed the bill making Yucca Mountain the nation's central repository for nuclear waste on July 23, 2002. Nevada's Republican governor, Kenny Guinn, and attorney general, Brian Sandoval, have sued Bush and the federal government to block the nuclear-dump plan. So far, strong opposition by politicians and citizens has delayed implementation, and the projected start date for the waste repository is uncertain.

In March 2006 the Bush administration requested additional funding for Yucca Mountain in order to facilitate the "nuclear renaissance." More allegations of shoddy quality-control work have been brought, this time concerning the corrosion rate of the waste packages. Because of these allegations, a stop-work order has been issued on that work. The nuclear industry is continuing its pressure to remove all obstacles to accelerating the building of new nuclear plants and has called for the 77,000-ton storage limit to be expanded.

In April 2006, because of the numerous quality-assurance issues, the opening date on Yucca Mountain was pushed back to 2020. In response Senator Pete Domenici (R-NM) threatened to introduce legislation to make changes in the project to ease industry concerns. On April 4 this legislation was introduced, and among other provisions, raises the ceiling on the amount of waste that will be accepted and opens the possibility of "interim" storage on the site (extracted from www.shundahai.org).

The late **CORBIN HARNEY** (1920–2007) was a member of the Western Shoshone Tribe of Duck Valley, Nevada. He was a healer and spiritual leader for his people, defender of Native American culture and rights, and an internationally known antinuclear activist. He founded the Shundahai Network in 1994 to promote visibility for Native American issues and opinions, and in 2003 he received the Nuclear-Free Future Award for his opposition to nuclear arms and atomic energy. He is also the founder of the Poohabah traditional healing center in Tecopa, California, near Death Valley.

ALEX PURBRICK managed Corbin Harney's speaking engagements and media interviews for four years, while she also filmed and photographed his activities and recorded his stories of his life. She currently lives in the Shetland Islands.